Collins

Physics

OCR
Gateway
GCSE

Revision
Guide

David Brodie

Revision

Contents

HT Higher Tier Content

Contents

HT Higher Tier Content

Contents

HT Higher Tier Content

Contents

HT Higher Tier Content

Review Questions

Recap of KS3 Key Concepts

1 In what form do hydroelectric generating systems store energy?

   A gravitational potential energy   C thermal energy

   B elastic potential energy   D internal energy   [1]

2 Which of these is **not** a unit of energy?

   A joule   B kilojoule   C kilowatt   D kilowatt-hour   [1]

3 Which of these **cannot** be detected by the human senses?

   A infrared radiation   C sound waves

   B radio waves   D visible light   [1]

4 Which of these is **not** part of the electromagnetic spectrum?

   A infrared radiation   C sound waves

   B radio waves   D visible light   [1]

5 Which of these forces requires contact?

   A electric force   C gravitational force

   B force of friction   D magnetic force   [1]

6 Which of these is a renewable energy resource?

   A coal   B gas   C oil   D wind   [1]

7 Which of these **always** happens during refraction?

   A waves pass from one medium into another   C light is absorbed

   B energy transfers   D frequency changes   [1]

8 What does an ammeter measure?

   A electric charge   C electric potential difference

   B electric current   D electrical resistance   [1]

9 Which of the following do atoms contain?

A only electrons

C only nuclei

B electrons and nuclei

D either electrons or nuclei   [1]

10 What is a device that uses magnetic force to create motion called?

A battery   B dynamo   C generator   D motor   [1]

11 The density of water is 1000kg/m³ and the density of aluminium is 2400kg/m³.

a) What is the mass of:

i) 1m³ of water?   ii) 1m³ of aluminium?   [2]

b) A bucket has a volume of 0.01m³. It is full to the brim with water.
What is the mass of the water?   [3]

c) If the same water is in the same bucket on the Moon, and none of it evaporates, what will be the mass of the water?   [1]

d) The bucket of water will be easier to carry on the Moon. Explain why this is.   [2]

e) What does evaporation of water from the bucket do to i) the mass of water,
ii) the volume of water, and iii) the density of water?   [3]

12 Match the words with their meanings by writing a list of pairs of letters and numbers.
For example: A2 is a correct answer.

A respiration   1 the light-sensing surface in your eye

B power   2 the process of getting energy from food and oxygen

C d.c.   3 the distance travelled by light in one year

D reflection   4 the rate of transfer of energy

E resistance   5 an electric current that stays in the same direction

F light-year   6 sound with frequency too high for human hearing

G retina   7 opposition to electric current

H ultrasound   8 the return of waves when hitting a surface   [8]

Total Marks _____ / 29

Matter, Models and Density

You must be able to:

- Explain that matter is made of atoms and describe the structure of an atom
- Understand that nuclei and electrons exert an electric force on each other
- Associate the different behaviours of solids, liquids and gases with differences in forces and distances between atoms and molecules
- Describe and calculate density.

A Simple Model of Atoms

- Matter is made of **atoms**.
- Sometimes an atom can be pictured as a very small ball – the ball is a **model** of an atom.

Inside Atoms – Electrons

- Every atom has even smaller **particles** inside it.
- J. J. Thomson discovered tiny particles with negative electric charge, called **electrons**.
- He suggested that electrons are embedded in atoms, like currants in a cake.
- He also knew that a whole atom is electrically neutral – with no overall **electric charge**.
- So the electrons must be balanced by a positive charge within each atom.
- Thomson suggested that the part of the atom with positive electric charge was like the soft 'sponge' of a cake.
- The cake is Thomson's model of an atom.

Inside Atoms – Nuclei

- Other scientists discovered small positively charged particles that come out from some kinds of radioactive material at very high speed. They called them **alpha particles**.
- Ernest Rutherford asked two of his students – Hans Geiger and Ernest Marsden – to fire some of these particles at very thin sheets of gold.
- They expected the alpha particles to shoot straight through the gold atoms, like bullets through cake.
- However, some bounced back. This is called **alpha scattering**.

> **Key Point**
>
> Atoms are very small – about 1×10^{-10}m in diameter. That's 0.1nm.

Models of Atoms

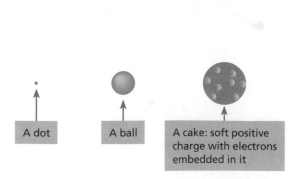

A dot

A ball

A cake: soft positive charge with electrons embedded in it

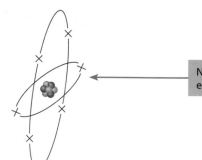

Nuclear atom: positive nucleus with electrons in orbit

- Atoms must contain something very dense and positively charged to cause the scattering.
- Rutherford concluded that the positive electric charge must be concentrated into a very tiny space deep inside each atom.
- He called this the **nucleus** of the atom.
- Niels Bohr, from Denmark, improved this nuclear model by describing the pathways of electrons in **orbit** around the nucleus.

Mass and Charge in Atoms

- The electric charge inside an atom is shared equally between the electrons (negative) and the nucleus (positive). But the nucleus has nearly all of the **mass**.
- Electric charge can cause **forces** between atoms.
- The forces hold atoms together to make solids and liquids.
- Some atoms can form groups held together by electric force. These groups are **molecules**.
- Water is made of molecules – each one has two hydrogen (H) atoms and one oxygen (O) atom, so water is H_2O.
- In gases, the forces between particles are very weak. So gases spread out into the space around them.
- Gases have much lower **density** than solids and liquids, e.g.
    - The density of air is approximately $1.2 kg/m^3$.
    - The density of solid iron is about $7800 kg/m^3$.
- Density is a **ratio** of mass to **volume**, i.e. mass is divided by volume to work out density.
- The unit of density is the kilogram per cubic metre (kg/m^3).

LEARN

$$\text{density } (kg/m^3) = \frac{\text{mass } (kg)}{\text{volume } (m^3)}$$

Particles in a Solid, Liquid and Gas

Gas

Liquid

Solid

Quick Test

1. State **three** facts about electrons.
2. Outline the evidence that led Rutherford to conclude that atoms have nuclei.
3. State the type of electric charge that nuclei have.
4. What holds the atoms of your body together?
5. Suggest why it is easy to walk through air but difficult to walk through walls.

Temperature and State

You must be able to:

* Understand that many materials can change between three states
* Explain that supplying energy to a material can change its internal energy by increasing its temperature or changing its state
* Define and make calculations using specific heat capacity
* Define and make calculations using specific latent heat.

Changes of State

* Some changes of state, e.g. melting (solid to liquid), **sublimating** (solid to gas) and boiling (liquid to gas), need the material to gain energy.
* For other changes of state, e.g. condensing (gas to liquid) and freezing (liquid to solid), the material loses energy.
* There is no change in the structures of atoms during a change of state.
* However, their energy and speed and the distance apart and force between them can change.
* Changes of state are not **chemical changes**. They are **physical changes**. They are **reversible**.
* The mass of material does not change during a change of state. Mass is **conserved**.
* Volume and density usually change during a change of state.
* The **internal energy** of a solid or liquid is linked to the forces between its atoms or molecules, as well as to the motion of the atoms or molecules.
* The internal energy of a gas is simpler. The forces between the atoms or molecules are insignificant, so internal energy is just the total kinetic energy of all of the atoms or molecules in the gas.

> **Key Point**
>
> Supplying energy to a material can increase its temperature or change its state.

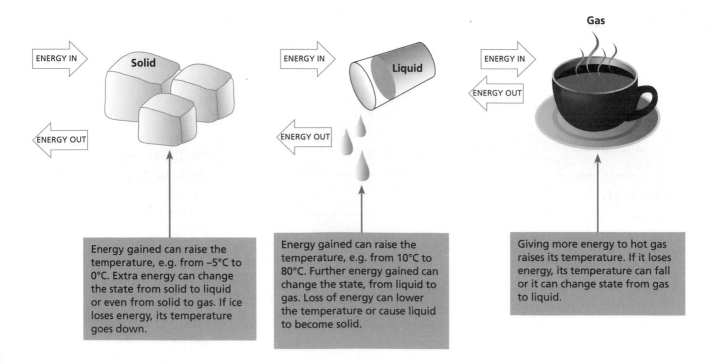

ENERGY IN | **Solid** | ENERGY OUT

Energy gained can raise the temperature, e.g. from −5°C to 0°C. Extra energy can change the state from solid to liquid or even from solid to gas. If ice loses energy, its temperature goes down.

ENERGY IN | **Liquid** | ENERGY OUT

Energy gained can raise the temperature, e.g. from 10°C to 80°C. Further energy gained can change the state, from liquid to gas. Loss of energy can lower the temperature or cause liquid to become solid.

Gas

ENERGY IN | ENERGY OUT

Giving more energy to hot gas raises its temperature. If it loses energy, its temperature can fall or it can change state from gas to liquid.

Specific Latent Heat

- The amount of energy needed to melt a substance is different for all substances, e.g.
  - It takes about 23 000 joules of energy to melt 1kg of lead.
  - It takes about 335 000 joules of energy to melt 1kg of ice.
- These values are called the **specific latent heat** of melting for lead and water – 23 000 joules per kilogram (J/kg) for lead and 335 000 J/kg for ice.
- A substance has a different value of specific latent heat for the change of state from liquid to gas. This is called the specific latent heat of vaporisation.

> **thermal energy for a change in state =**
>
> **mass × specific latent heat**

Specific Heat Capacity

- Energy isn't just needed for a change of state. It is also needed to raise the temperature of a material.
- It takes about 450J to raise the temperature of 1kg of iron by 1°C (or by 1K).
- It takes about 4200J to raise the temperature of 1kg of water by 1°C (or 1K).
- These values are the **specific heat capacities** of iron and water – 450J/kg°C for iron and 4200J/kg°C for water.
- The specific heat capacity of a material is the energy needed to raise the temperature of 1kg by 1°C (or 1K).

> **change in thermal energy =**
>
> **mass × specific heat capacity × change in temperature**

 Key Point

Temperature can be measured in degrees Celsius (°C), or in kelvin (K). Zero kelvin is the lowest possible temperature. Ice melts at 0°C or 273K. Water boils at 100°C or 373K. A temperature difference of 1°C is the same as a difference of 1K.

Key Point

We can predict the energy needed for temperature change if we know the specific heat capacity of the material and its mass.

 Quick Test

1. Name **one** quantity that changes when a substance changes state and **one** quantity that does not change.
2. Explain whether or not temperature always changes when a substance gains energy.
3. If the specific latent heat of melting of iron is 267 000J/kg, calculate how much energy will be needed to melt 1 tonne (1000kg).
4. If the specific heat capacity of air is 1006J/kg°C, calculate how much energy will be needed to raise the temperature of a room containing 100kg of air by 10°C (if none of the air escapes).

 Key Words

sublimate
chemical change
physical change
reversible
conserved
internal energy
specific latent heat
specific heat capacity

Pressure

You must be able to:

- Explain that gas pressure is caused by gas molecules bombarding surfaces
- Use your understanding of particles to explain the effects of changing the volume, temperature and pressure of gases
- HT Calculate pressure in liquids
- Recall that *g* is the Earth's gravitational field strength and is approximately 10N/kg.

Gas Pressure

- A gas in a box exerts **pressure** on all of the walls of the box because its molecules **bombard** the walls.
- Most gases have atoms in small groups or molecules. This includes oxygen and hydrogen, where each molecule is a pair of atoms.
- Pressure is force acting on each square area, such as a square metre.
- Pressure is measured in pascals (Pa).

 LEARN

$$\text{pressure (Pa)} = \frac{\text{force normal to a surface (N)}}{\text{area of that surface (m}^2)}$$

- The overall pressure that the gas exerts is at right-angles to the walls.

> **Key Point**
>
> The smallest particles in most gases are molecules, which are made of more than one atom. Molecules in a gas move at high speed with little or no force between them.

Gas Pressure, Volume and Temperature

- The faster the particles in a gas move, the bigger the pressure. So pressure is related to temperature.
- If the box is made smaller:
  - the particles become closer together and the walls are hit more often by the gas molecules
  - there is more pressure on the walls, so pressure also depends on the volume of the box.
- Applying pressure to a gas can reduce its volume. The gas is **compressed**.
- Reducing pressure on the gas can make it **expand**.

HT In devices such as bicycle pumps:
  - the force needed and the compression of the gas mean that energy is supplied to the gas
  - the energy can increase the temperature of the gas, so the bicycle pump can get hot.

Molecular Bombardment and Gas Pressure

Gas molecules bombard surfaces and create pressure.

Space and Atmosphere

- Space is a **vacuum**.
- High in the Earth's **atmosphere**, close to space, the gas particles are far apart, so they exert little pressure.
- Lower in the atmosphere the particles are closer together and make more collisions with each other and with everything else.

Pressure in Liquids

HT An object in a liquid also experiences pressure.

HT This is due to the **weight** of liquid above the object.

HT The pressure acts at right-angles to every surface, not just downwards.

HT At greater depths in liquid, there is more liquid above the object, so there is greater pressure.

> **pressure due to a column of liquid (Pa) =**
> **height of column (m) × density of liquid (kg/m³) × g (N/kg)**

- Gravitational field strength (g), is close to 10N/kg at the Earth's surface.
- This means that every mass of 1kg experiences a force of gravity (weight) of 10 newtons (N).

HT Upthrust, Floating and Sinking

- An object experiences more pressure on its lower surface than on its upper surface.

> **pressure difference at two points in a liquid =**
> **depth difference of the two points × density of liquid × g**

- This pressure difference creates an upward force on the object, called **upthrust**.
- If the weight of the object is greater than the upthrust, it will sink.
- If the weight of the object is smaller than the upthrust, it will rise to the surface.

 Key Point

A body floats on the surface of a liquid, partly submerged, when its weight is equal to the upwards force of the liquid (upthrust).

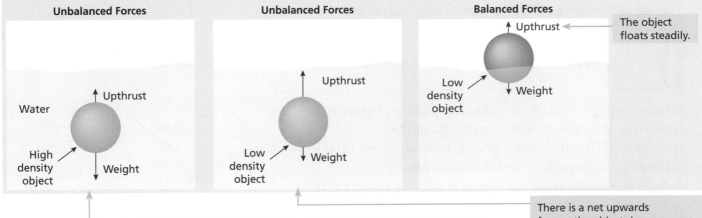

The object floats steadily.

There is a net upwards force – the object rises.

There is a net downwards force – the object sinks.

Quick Test

1. Use ideas about molecules to explain why increasing the temperature of a gas (but keeping its volume the same) causes an increase in pressure.
2. Use ideas about molecules to explain why increasing the volume of a gas (but keeping its temperature the same) causes a decrease in pressure.
3. Describe how density of the atmosphere changes with height above the Earth.
4. **HT** Use ideas about forces to explain why :
   a) some objects sink
   b) some objects float (partly below and partly above the liquid level).

Key Words

pressure
bombard
compress
expand
vacuum
atmosphere
HT weight
HT upthrust

Journeys

You must be able to:

- Make measurements and calculations of speed, time and distance
- Calculate the kinetic energy of a moving body
- Understand the importance of vector quantities (displacement, velocity and acceleration) when considering motion
- Interpret displacement–time and velocity–time graphs
- Calculate acceleration.

Speed and Velocity

- Miles per hour (mph) can be used to measure the speed of vehicles.
- However, in the standard international **SI system**, metres per second (m/s) is used.
- 1 m/s is equal to 3.6 kilometres per hour (km/h or kph) and 2.24 mph.
- Distance and speed are **scalar quantities** (without direction).
- They are used when direction is not important.
- When thinking about energy, direction is not important.
- The energy of a moving body is called **kinetic energy**, which is measured in joules (J).

> **kinetic energy (J) = 0.5 × mass (kg) × (speed (m/s))²**

- This equation can be used for predicting journeys:

> **distance travelled (m) = speed (m/s) × time (s)**

- When direction is important, **displacement** and **velocity** are used.
- Quantities with direction are **vector quantities**.
- Arrows of different lengths and directions can be used to compare different displacements and different velocities.
- A negative vector quantity means it is in the reverse direction.

$$\text{velocity} = \frac{\text{displacement}}{\text{time}}$$

Key Point

You must be able to rearrange the distance equation to work out speed and time, i.e.

$$\text{speed} = \frac{\text{distance}}{\text{time}}$$

$$\text{time} = \frac{\text{distance}}{\text{Speed}}$$

If the speed on a journey varies, the average speed is given by the total distance divided by the total time.

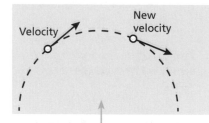

An object moving in a curved path with constant speed has a changing velocity, because the direction of motion is changing.

Graphs of Journeys

- Displacement–time graphs can be used to describe journeys.
- The **slope or gradient** of a displacement–time graph is equal to velocity.

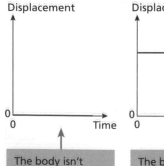

The body isn't moving.

The body isn't moving.

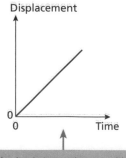

The body is moving steadily. It has constant velocity.

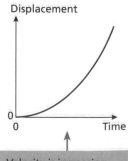

Velocity is increasing. The body is accelerating.

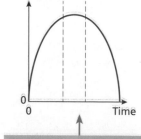

The body turns around and returns to where it started.

- Velocity–time graphs can be used to describe the same journeys.

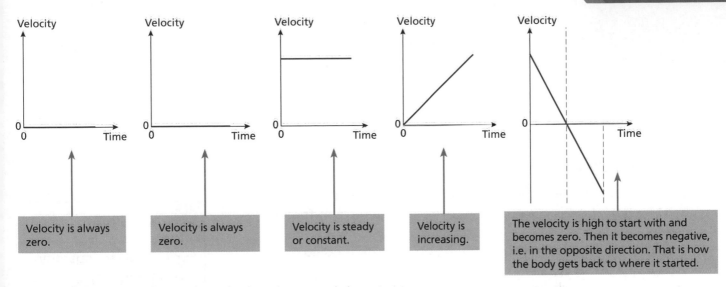

| Velocity is always zero. | Velocity is always zero. | Velocity is steady or constant. | Velocity is increasing. | The velocity is high to start with and becomes zero. Then it becomes negative, i.e. in the opposite direction. That is how the body gets back to where it started. |

- The slope or gradient of a velocity–time graph is equal to acceleration.
- **HT** The enclosed area under a velocity–time graph is equal to displacement.

Acceleration

- **Acceleration** is rate of change of velocity. It is a vector quantity.

LEARN

$$\text{acceleration (m/s}^2\text{)} = \frac{\text{change in velocity (m/s)}}{\text{time (s)}}$$

$$(\text{final velocity (m/s)})^2 - (\text{initial velocity (m/s)})^2 = 2 \times \text{acceleration (m/s}^2\text{)} \times \text{distance (m)}$$

- When an object is released close to the Earth's surface, it accelerates downwards.
- Then the acceleration is approximately $10\,\text{m/s}^2$. This is called **acceleration due to gravity**, or acceleration of free fall, (g).

Quick Test

1. Calculate the kinetic energy, in joules (J), of a ball of mass 0.5kg moving at 16m/s.
2. Calculate how long a 100km journey would take at an average speed of 40kph.
3. Calculate the acceleration, in m/s^2, of a car that goes from standstill (0m/s) to 24m/s in 10s.
4. Suggest what the acceleration of a ball that is dropped to the ground would be.

Key Words

SI system
scalar quantity
kinetic energy
displacement
velocity
vector quantity
slope
gradient
acceleration
acceleration due to
  gravity (g)

Forces

You must be able to:

- Calculate combinations of forces that act along the same line
- Understand that forces act in pairs of the same size but opposite direction
- Recall that acceleration is not possible without net force, and a net force always produces acceleration.

Contact Force

- You can push and pull objects by making contact with them.
- The force you apply can be partly or completely a force of **friction**.
- Friction acts parallel to the surface of the object.
- You can also push at right-angles to the object. This is called a **normal force**.
- Force is measured in newtons, N.

Non-Contact Force

- Two magnets can attract or **repel** each other without touching.
- Electric force also acts without contact (without touching).
- Gravity provides another force that can act at a distance.

Gravitational and Electric Force

- All objects that have mass experience gravitational force.
- All objects with electric charge experience electric force.
- Gravitational force is always attractive, so there must be only one kind of mass.
- The Earth attracts you. The force, measured in N, is your weight.
- Electric force can be attractive or repulsive, so there must be two kinds of electric charge – positive and negative.

Net Force

- The overall force for a combination of forces is called their **resultant force** or **net force**.
- When there is a net force on an object it *always* accelerates.
- When there is no force at all on an object or the forces are balanced, it *never* accelerates. (It can move, but the motion never changes.)
- A body stays still or keeps moving at constant velocity unless an **external force** acts on it. That idea is called **Newton's first law**.

Direction of Force

- The direction of a force makes a big difference to the effect it has.
  - Two forces of the same size acting in opposite directions do *not* cause acceleration, so the net force is zero.
  - Two forces acting in the same direction add together to produce a bigger net force.

> **Key Point**
>
> Force is a vector quantity – direction matters. Arrows can be drawn to show forces.

> **Key Point**
>
> If net force is not zero, the forces are unbalanced and there is acceleration. If motion is steady and in a straight line, velocity is constant and there is no acceleration.

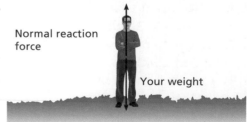

Normal reaction force

Your weight

- When you push an object, you experience a force of the same size and in the opposite direction.
- **Newton's third law** states that for every force there is an equal and opposite force.
- For example, a spacecraft can accelerate (or decelerate) by pushing gases (made by burning fuel) away from itself.
- When you stand on the floor:
  - your weight acts as a force on the floor
  - the floor provides an equal force in the opposite direction – this is called a normal reaction force.

Force and Acceleration

- Net force is related to acceleration in a fairly simple way:
  - acceleration is bigger when force is bigger
  - but smaller when mass is bigger.

LEARN

force (N) = mass (kg) × acceleration (m/s²)

- This equation is a form of **Newton's second law.**

> ### Key Point
>
> The bigger the mass of an object, the greater the force needed to produce an acceleration. An object with more mass has more inertia, so it is more difficult to change its velocity.

HT Resistive Force on a Falling Object

- Air resistance creates a **resistive force** opposite to the force of gravity.
- The faster an object falls, the bigger the resistive force.
- Eventually the upwards resistive force becomes as big as the downwards gravitational force.
- The two forces are equal and opposite, so there is no net force.
- When there is no net force there is no acceleration, so a falling object continues to fall at constant velocity.
- That velocity is called the object's **terminal velocity.**

At first velocity is small so resistive force is small. There is a large net force acting downwards. The skydiver accelerates downwards.

As velocity increases, resistive force increases. But there is still a net downwards force so the skydiver continues to gain velocity.

Eventually, the velocity is so large that resistive force is the same size as the weight. Net force is zero. So acceleration is zero. Velocity stays the same.

> ### Key Words
>
> friction
> normal force
> repel
> resultant force
> net force
> external force
> Newton's first law
> Newton's third law
> Newton's second law
> HT resistive force
> HT terminal velocity

Quick Test

1. Name the kind of force that keeps you in your seat.
2. Name the kind of force that holds your body together.
3. State what is necessary, in terms of forces, for acceleration to happen.
4. HT When a ball is dropped, the effect of air resistance is ignored because it is so small. Explain why a skydiver, who jumps from a plane, cannot ignore the effect of air resistance.

Force, Energy and Power

You must be able to:

- Select from a range of equations so that you can analyse and predict motion
- **HT** Understand what momentum is and that it is conserved in collisions
- Understand 'doing work' as mechanical energy transfer.

HT Momentum

- **Momentum** is the product of mass and velocity. It is a vector quantity, so direction is important.

LEARN
> **momentum (kgm/s) = mass (kg) × velocity (m/s)**

- Whenever bodies collide, their total momentum is the same before and after the collision – it is **conserved**.

LEARN
> **total momentum before = total momentum after**

Force, Work and Energy

- When a force acts and a body accelerates as a result of this force, energy is supplied to the body.
- We say that the force does **work** on the body.
- The amount of work done and the energy supplied to the body are the same:

LEARN
> **work done (J) = energy supplied =
> force × distance (m) (along the line of action of the force)**

- The unit of energy is the joule (J).

> **1J = 1N × 1m**

- Work must be done to overcome **friction** as well as to cause acceleration.
- When there is friction, some or all of the energy causes heating.
- In some situations, some of the work done increases an object's **potential energy**.

LEARN
> **(in a gravity field) potential energy (J) =
> mass (kg) × height (m) × gravitational field strength, g (N/kg)**

Energy Stores and Transfers

- Energy can be stored in different ways, e.g.
  - in the **kinetic energy** of a moving body
  - as **gravitational potential energy**
  - as **elastic potential energy**
  - as **thermal energy**.
- Energy can be taken from these stores and transferred to other systems.
- Sometimes the energy becomes thinly spread out and only heats the surroundings of a process. Then it cannot be usefully transferred.

> **energy transferred (J) = charge (C) × potential difference (V)**

- Wasted energy **dissipates** in the surroundings.

Power

- Energy can be transferred quickly or slowly.
- The rate of transfer of energy is **power**.

> **power (W) = rate of transfer of energy (J/s)**
> $$= \frac{\text{energy (J)}}{\text{time (s)}}$$

- Doing work is one way of transferring energy. It is energy transfer involving force and distance.
- So, when work is done:

> **power (W) =** $\dfrac{\text{work done (J)}}{\text{time (s)}}$

Revise

Key Point

A bow and arrow, with the bowstring pulled back, is an example of an energy storage system. It's an elastic potential energy store.

Key Words

HT **momentum**
HT **conserved**
work
friction
potential energy
kinetic energy
gravitational potential energy
elastic potential energy
thermal energy
dissipate
power

Quick Test

1. HT Two balls of the same mass and with the same speed collide head on. State and explain what their total momentum is before the collision, and what their total momentum is after the collision.
2. An ice skater can move in a straight line at almost constant speed without needing to supply more energy. Explain, in terms of force and distance, how that is possible.
3. When you lean against a wall you are not doing work. Explain why in terms of force and distance.
4. Describe the relationship between power and energy.

Changes of Shape

You must be able to:

- Distinguish between plastic and elastic materials
- Distinguish between linear and non-linear relationships
- Understand that for a linear relationship, the slope or gradient is constant
- Recall that a planet's gravitational field strength depends on its mass.

Extension and Compression

- A pair of forces acting outwards on an object can stretch it, or **extend** it, even if the forces are balanced and there is no acceleration.
- A pair of forces acting inwards on an object can **compress** it.
- Combinations of forces can also bend objects.
- Change of shape can be called **deformation**.

Elastic and Plastic Deformation

- When forces make an object change shape, but it returns to its original shape when the forces are removed, the deformation is said to be **elastic**.
- If the object keeps its new shape when the deforming forces are removed, the deformation is **plastic**.

Extension of Springs

- A spring experiences elastic deformation unless the force applied is large. Then the spring may be permanently stretched.
- For a spring, unless the force is very large, the amount of extension is **proportional to** the size of the deforming force.
- When the force changes, the amount of the extension changes by the same proportion.
- A graph of extension and applied force is a straight line – the relationship between force and extension is **linear.**

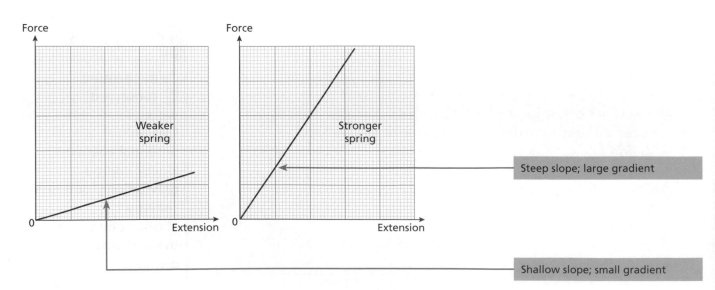

- The gradient of the graph is different for individual springs. It is called the **spring constant**.

> force exerted on a spring (N) =
> extension (m) × spring constant (N/m)

- The graph produced by a rubber band is not a straight line. The relationship is **non-linear.**

Energy Stored by a Stretched Spring

- Stretching a spring involves force and distance (the extension) in the same direction. So work must be done to stretch a spring.

> work done = average force × distance = $\left(\dfrac{\text{final force}}{2}\right)$ × distance
>
> work done = energy transferred in stretching (J) =
> $0.5 \times$ spring constant (N/m) $\times$ (extension (m))^2

Mass and Weight

- In Physics, we treat **weight** as a type of force, so we measure it in newtons (N). It is the force on an object due to gravity.
- Different **planets** and **moons** have different **gravitational field strengths**, g, at their surface. This means that objects have different weights on different planets and moons.
- Weight is related to mass:

> weight = gravity force (N) =
> mass (kg) × gravitational field strength, g (N/kg)

- On Earth, $g = 10$N/kg; on the Moon, $g = 1.6$N/kg; near the surface of Jupiter, $g = 26$N/kg.

Quick Test

1. A pair of forces that act on an object along the same line are balanced (equal size, opposite direction) and cannot accelerate the object. What effect can they have?
2. State which of the following show **elastic** behaviour and which show **plastic** behaviour:
   a) a guitar string
   b) a piece of modelling clay
   c) a saw blade when it is flicked
   d) a saw blade when a large force bends it permanently.
3. Physics distinguishes between mass and weight and uses different units (kg for mass and N for weight). Explain why this distinction is generally not used in everyday life.

Key Words

extend
compress
deformation
elastic
plastic
proportional to
linear
spring constant
non-linear
weight
planet
moon
gravitational field
  strength (g)

Levers, Gears and Hydraulic Systems

You must be able to:

- Calculate the moment of a force and apply this to understanding levers
- Understand that for a balanced (non-rotating) object, total clockwise moments and total anticlockwise moments are equal
- Recall that a lever can multiply force but not energy
- Recall that gears and hydraulic systems can also multiply force.

Moments Around a Pivot

- Pairs of forces that act along different lines can make bodies **rotate**.
- A **pivot** can provide force.
- Another force, acting at a different point, can cause rotation around the pivot. This is an **applied force**.
- The turning effect of the applied force is called its **moment**.

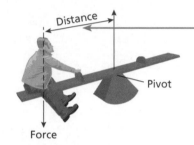

Distance

Pivot

Force

> The bigger the distance from the pivot, the bigger the turning effect.

- The moment can be clockwise or anticlockwise around the pivot.
- The size of the moment depends on:
  - the force
  - the shortest distance from the line of the force to the pivot.

> **LEARN**
> **moment of a force (Nm) =**
> **force (N) × distance (m) (normal to the direction of the force)**

Key Point
The turning effect of the applied force, relative to the pivot, is called its moment.

- The unit of moment is the newton-metre (Nm).
- This distance is at right-angles to the force.

Balanced Objects

- If total clockwise moments and total anticlockwise moments are equal, the body is balanced.
- This is sometimes called the **principle of moments**.

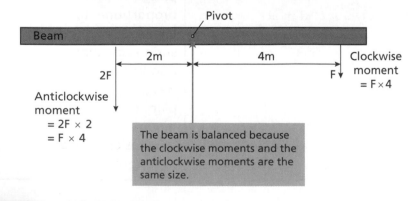

Pivot

Beam

2m   4m   Clockwise moment = F × 4

2F

F

Anticlockwise moment
= 2F × 2
= F × 4

> The beam is balanced because the clockwise moments and the anticlockwise moments are the same size.

Key Point
The principle of moments states that if a body is balanced the sum of the clockwise moments and the sum of the anticlockwise moments are in opposite direction and also equal in size.

Levers

- Because distance is important, a smaller force can 'beat' a bigger force.
- A **lever** can **multiply** the applied force to move a **load**, but the applied force must move through a bigger distance.
- A lever cannot multiply energy.

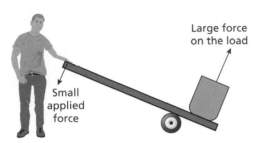

Large force on the load

Small applied force

Gears

- **Gears** can also use a smaller force to overcome a bigger force.
- If two **cogs** of different sizes are engaged together, the smaller cog makes more turns (or revolutions) for each turn of the bigger one.
- A small force applied to turn the smaller cog can act on a bigger load, through the bigger cog.

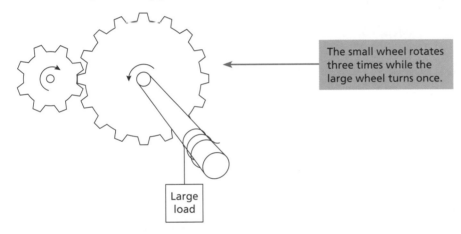

The small wheel rotates three times while the large wheel turns once.

Large load

Hydraulic Systems

- A **hydraulic system** can also multiply force.
- A hydraulic system – filled with liquid – can have a pair of **pistons**.
- A small force applied to a small piston with small area produces pressure, which is transmitted without reduction to a larger area.
- The force acting on a bigger piston is bigger than the applied force.

A Hydraulic System

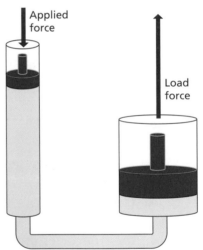

Applied force

Load force

Key Words

rotate
pivot
applied force
moment
principle of moments
lever
multiply
load
gear
cog
hydraulic system
piston

> **Quick Test**
>
> 1. Explain why a force acting at a pivot has no turning effect.
> 2. Outline the principle of moments.
> 3. Levers can multiply force (the applied force is smaller than the load). Explain why the point at which the force is applied must move through a larger distance than the load.
> 4. Use the relationship between force and pressure to explain how a hydraulic system multiplies force.

Practice Questions

Matter, Models and Density

1 Which of these is a unit of volume?

    A m   **B** m^2 **C** m^3 **D** m^4 [1]

2 Complete the sentence.

An atom must be electrically neutral if:

    A it is an ion.

    B it is a molecule.

    C it has equal numbers of protons and neutrons.

    D it has equal numbers of protons and electrons.   [1]

3 What is the approximate size of an atom?

    A 1×10^{10}m   **B** 1×10^{0}m   **C** 1×10^{-1}m   **D** 1×10^{-10}m   [1]

4 How is density calculated?

    A mass × volume   **B** $\dfrac{\text{mass}}{\text{volume}}$ **C** $\dfrac{\text{volume}}{\text{mass}}$ [1]

5 Why are gases less dense than solids and liquids?

    A their particles are further apart   **C** their particles are smaller

    B their particles are closer together   **D** their particles are bigger   [1]

6 An object has a mass of 0.24kg and a volume of $0.0001m^3$.

What is the density of the object?   [3]

7 The 'cake' model and the nuclear model of the atom both describe positive and negative charge and the mass of the atom.

    a) Where is the positive charge in:

        i) the nuclear model?   [1]

        ii) the cake model?   [1]

b) Where is the negative charge in:

   i) the nuclear model? [2]

   ii) the cake model? [2]

c) Where is most of the mass of the atom in:

   i) the nuclear model? [1]

   ii) the cake model? [1]

Total Marks .... / 16

Temperature and State

1 Which of these is **not** a change of state?

  A evaporation   **C** boiling

  B expansion   **D** sublimation [1]

2 Which word describes what happens when pressure is applied to a gas to reduce its volume?

  A compression   **C** evaporation

  B expansion   **D** sublimation [1]

3 Which of the following best describes how the internal energy of a sample of material can be changed?

  A only by change of state

  B only by change of temperature

  C by change of state or change of temperature. [1]

4 Sort the following processes into **two** sets: those that require (or take in) energy and those that release (or give out) energy. [5]

    boiling   **condensing**   **evaporation**   **freezing**   **melting**

5 Describe what happens to the particles in a gas when it is heated. [2]

6 When a liquid is heated, what can happen to its particles? [3]

7 Why does scalding from steam at 100°C cause more pain and worse damage than
   a scald from water at 100°C? [2]

8 a) What additional information, as well as specific latent heat, is needed to calculate
       the amount of energy required to melt an ice cube? [1]

   b) What additional information, as well as the change in temperature, is needed to
       calculate the amount of energy that must be given to water in a pan to heat it
       (without it changing state)? [2]

> **Total Marks** .... / 18

Pressure

1 What happens to the pressure of a gas if its volume increases but the temperature stays the same?

   A it decreases   C it stays the same

   B it increases   D it's not possible to predict [1]

2 HT What water pressure acts on a submarine at a depth of 50m if the density of sea water
       is 1024kg/m³?
       pressure = density of liquid × g × depth of liquid [1]

   A 51.2Pa   B 51.2kPa   C 512Pa   D 512kPa

3 a) Explain why a gas exerts more pressure if its temperature increases and its volume stays
       the same. [2]

   b) If the temperature of a gas increases a little, but the volume changes a lot, then
       the pressure can decrease.

       Explain why this is. [2]

4 HT a) Why does the pressure exerted by a liquid increase with depth? [1]

       b) How does this explain why bodies experience an upwards force in water? [3]

> **Total Marks** .... / 10

Journeys

1 Which of these is **not** a unit of speed?

   A mph   **B** km/h   **C** m/s   **D** kg/s   [1]

2 How far can you walk in 3 hours at an average speed of 4km/h?

   A 0.75km   **B** 1.33km   **C** 7km   **D** 12km   [1]

3 Which of these is a unit of energy?

   A joule   **B** newton   **C** pascal   **D** watt   [1]

4 What happens to the speed of the Earth as it orbits the Sun?

   A it decreases

   B it stays the same

   C it increases

   D it changes direction   [1]

5 HT What happens to the velocity of the Earth as it orbits the Sun?

      A it decreases

      B it stays the same

      C it increases

      D it changes direction   [1]

6 How far can you travel in 1 hour at an average speed of:

   a) 24km/h?   [3]

   b) 40mph?   [2]

   c) 4m/s?   [3]

   d) i) Give your answer to part **a)** in metres.   [1]

      ii) Give your answer to part **b)** in metres.   [2]
        1mile = 1.6km = 1600m

7 Volume is a scalar quantity but force is a vector quantity.

a) What is the difference between a vector and a scalar quantity? [1]

b) Give another example of a vector quantity. [1]

c) Give another example of a scalar quantity. [1]

8 A plane takes off in Hong Kong and lands in London 12 hours later. The distance of the journey is 6000km.

a) What is its average speed in km/h? [3]

b) What is its average speed in m/s? [2]

c) HT For most of the flight, speed does not change much, but velocity does.

In what way does the velocity change? [2]

9 HT A spaceship can keep travelling in a straight line without slowing down.

a) Why can't a car do the same? [1]

b) How does a spaceship accelerate? [1]

Total Marks _____ / 28

Forces

1 Which of these forces requires contact?

A electric or electrostatic force

B frictional force

C gravitational force

D magnetic force [1]

2 Which graph shows acceleration?

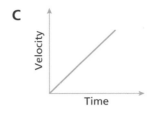

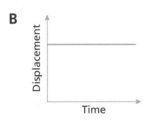

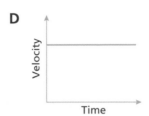

[1]

3 HT What always produces resistance to acceleration?

    A energy   **B** mass   **C** pressure   **D** velocity   [1]

4 If a ball is kicked along the ground it eventually slows down and stops, i.e. it decelerates.

What force causes this deceleration? [1]

5 What does Newton's first law say about force? [1]

6 What does Newton's third law say about force? [1]

Total Marks _____ / 6

Force, Energy and Power

1 Which of these is necessary for doing work?

A energy   **B** mass   **C** pressure   **D** velocity   [1]

2 If the point of a pin has an area of $1 \times 10^{-7}m^2$, how much pressure does it exert on a surface when it is pushed with a force of 10N?

A 10^8Pa   **B** 10^{-6}Pa   **C** 10^6Pa   **D** 10^8Pa   [1]

Total Marks _____ / 2

Changes of Shape

1 What word describes the behaviour of a material that keeps its new shape after a deforming force is removed?

   A elastic

   B plastic

   C compressed

   D extended   [1]

2 Here are four force-extension graphs, with the same scales on both axes, for four different springs.

Which graph has the biggest spring constant?

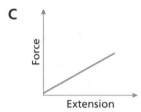

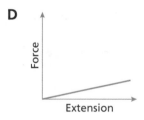

[1]

3 In physics, which is the correct statement about weight?

   A Weight is a quantity measured in kilograms (kg).

   B Weight is a quantity measured in joules (J).

   C Weight is the force of gravity.

   D Weight is the gravitational field strength.   [1]

Total Marks _____ / 3

Levers, Gears and Hydraulic Systems

1 What is the turning effect of a force called?

   A moment

   B pivot

   C pressure

   D work   [1]

2 What is a hydraulic system filled with?

   A gas because it transmits pressure

   B gas because it doesn't transmit pressure

   C liquid because it transmits pressure

   D liquid because it doesn't transmit pressure   [1]

3 **a)** What is the moment of a force of 18N that acts 1.5m from a pivot?   [3]

   b) If this force is the applied force acting on a lever, what will be the force that acts on a load placed 0.3m from the pivot?   [3]

4 Describe the effects of the forces on the beam in each of the following examples:

   a)

                                   [1]

   b)

                                   [1]

   c)

                                   [1]

Total Marks _____ / 11

Electric Charge

You must be able to:

- Recall that in everyday objects there are many atoms, each with electrons
- Recall that friction can transfer some electrons from one object to another, so that both objects become charged
- Understand that electric current in metal conductors, including wires, is a result of the flow of large numbers of electrons
- Understand that resistance to current produces heat, which transfers energy from the circuit to the surroundings.

Electric Force and Electric Charge

- Electric force can be attractive or repulsive and can act at a distance.
- Electric force acts between bodies that have net charge.
- There are two types of charge – positive and negative.
- When many charged particles, such as electrons, move together they form an **electric current**.
- In a **neutral** atom, the negative charge of the electrons is balanced by the positive charge of the nucleus.
- The unit of charge is the coulomb (C).

Electrostatic Phenomena

- Forces between objects much larger than atoms can be observed when there is an imbalance of positive and negative charge.
- The observations, or **phenomena**, are called static electricity, or **electrostatics**, because the charged particles are not flowing.
- Friction can **transfer** electrons from one object to another:
  - one object will have an excess of electrons and a negative charge
  - the other object will have a shortage of electrons and a positive charge.
- The space around a charged object is called its **electric field**.

Electric Field Lines Around a Single Positive Charge

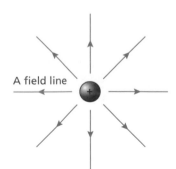

A field line

Electric Field Lines Around One Positive and One Negative Charge

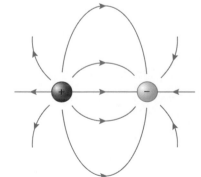

 The arrows show the direction of the force that can act on a small positive charge in different places.

Sparks

- A very strong electric field can cause particles of air to separate into electrons and 'atoms' with a shortage of electrons.
- These charged 'atoms' are positive **ions**.
- The electric field can accelerate the charged particles.
- When there is a lot of movement of charge between the objects, the air sparks.

Electric Current

- Metals are **conductors** of electricity.
- When many electrons move in the same direction in a wire, there is an electric current.
- Electric current inside a closed loop of wire can be continuous if the electrons experience continuous force from a source of energy.
- **Batteries** and **cells**, for example, can create continuous force.
- **Ammeters** are used to measure current.
- They are connected into circuits so that the circuit current flows through them.
- Current is measured in amperes or amps (A).
- Current is equal to rate of flow of charge:

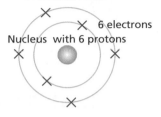

A Neutral Atom

6 electrons
Nucleus with 6 protons

A Positive Ion

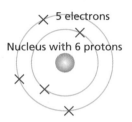

5 electrons
Nucleus with 6 protons

$$current (A) = \frac{charge\ flow\ (C)}{time\ (s)}$$

$$charge\ flow\ (C) = current\ (A) \times time\ (s)$$

- Unless it is isolated (cut off) from other objects, a conductor cannot keep excess electric charge, because electrons flow in or out of it too easily.

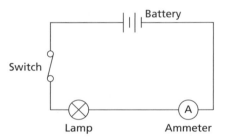

Battery

Switch

Lamp   Ammeter

For a current to flow in this circuit there must be an energy supply and a complete loop (or closed circuit).

Resistance

- Current can flow through an electrical conductor, such as a metal wire, but there is always some **resistance** to the flow.
- This resistance means that a wire can be heated by an electrical current. Energy passes from the wire to the surroundings.
- Resistance is measured in ohms (Ω).

Quick Test

1. What are the two types of electric force?
2. a) Outline how an object, such as an inflated balloon, becomes electrically charged.
   b) Explain why it is **not** possible to charge a metal spoon in the same way as the balloon.
3. What is the difference between charge and current?
4. Describe how resistance causes transfer of energy from a circuit.

Key Words

electric current
neutral
phenomenon
electrostatics
transfer
electric field
ion
conductor
battery
cell
ammeter
resistance

Circuits

You must be able to:

- Understand that resistance to current produces heat, which transfers energy from the circuit to the surroundings
- Understand that a potential difference, or voltage, is needed to keep a current going around a circuit
- Investigate the relationship between current and voltage for different components.

Circuits and Symbols

- A system of symbols is used to represent the different **components** in circuits.
- The components in electrical circuits can be connected in **series** or in **parallel** (see pages 36–37)

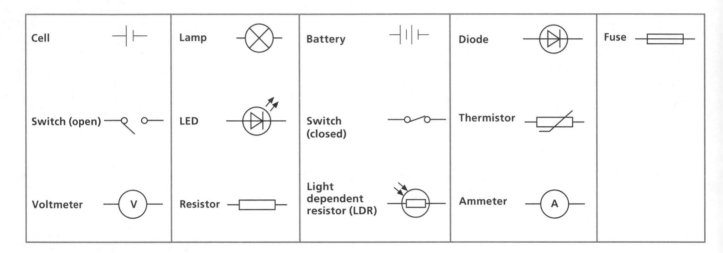

Cell	Lamp	Battery	Diode	Fuse
Switch (open)	LED	Switch (closed)	Thermistor	
Voltmeter	Resistor	Light dependent resistor (LDR)	Ammeter	

Potential Difference or Voltage

- Batteries and other power supplies can replace the energy that is transferred out of the wires and components in a circuit.
- Batteries and other power supplies only work when they are part of a circuit.
- A battery has a **positive terminal** (which attracts negative charge, so it attracts electrons) and a **negative terminal** (which repels negative charge).
- The abilities of batteries or other power supplies to provide energy to moving charge in a circuit can be compared using **potential difference** or **voltage**.
- Potential difference or voltage is measured in volts (V).

> **LEARN**
> energy transferred (J) = charge (C) × potential difference (V)

- **Voltmeters** are used to measure voltage.
- A voltmeter is connected to two points. The circuit current does not flow through a voltmeter.

> **Key Point**
>
> For continuous current, a continuous potential difference and a continuous loop of conductor (such as wire and other components) are necessary.

> **Key Point**
>
> The potential difference between two points in a circuit is 1V if 1J of energy is transferred when 1C of charge passes between the points.

Current, Potential Difference and Resistance

- An increase in potential difference can increase the current in a circuit.
- An increase in resistance in a circuit can decrease the current.

> **LEARN**
>
> $$\text{current (A)} = \frac{\text{potential difference (V)}}{\text{resistance } (\Omega)}$$
>
> $$\text{potential difference (V)} = \text{current (A)} \times \text{resistance } (\Omega)$$

Current–Voltage Relationships

- If the temperature of a metal wire doesn't change, its resistance doesn't change.
  - Current is proportional to voltage.
  - A current–voltage (I–V) graph is a straight line that passes through the **origin** of the graph.
  - The relationship between current and voltage is linear.
- For a wire that gets hotter as voltage and current get bigger, the resistance increases and the relationship between current and voltage is non-linear.
- This happens in a filament lamp, in which the wire is white hot.
- A **thermistor** behaves in the opposite way to a wire.
- As it becomes hotter, more electrons become free to move, so its resistance goes down.
- For a thermistor the current–voltage relationship is also non-linear.
- Thermistors are sensitive to changes in temperature.
- This means thermistors can be used as electrical temperature **sensors**.
- **Diodes** and **Light Dependent Resistors (LDRs)** also have non-linear current–voltage relationships.
- Diodes only allow current in one direction. When a voltage is in the 'reverse' direction, no current flows.
- For LDRs, when the light intensity increases the resistance goes down.

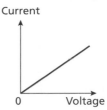

A voltmeter measures a difference between two points in a circuit.

Wire with Little Heating

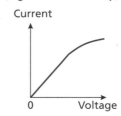

A Wire That Gets Hot at a Higher Voltage (e.g. A Filament Lamp)

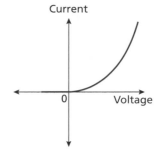

Diode (Reverse Voltage Produces Zero Current)

> ## Quick Test
>
> 1. Explain why a voltmeter is connected to two points in a circuit that are separated by a component, such as a resistor.
> 2. Outline what can cause the current in a simple circuit to **a)** increase and **b)** decrease.
> 3. Explain why a current–voltage graph for a wire becomes curved when the wire becomes hot.
> 4. What happens to the resistance of a thermistor when its temperature increases?

> ## Key Words
>
> component
> series
> parallel
> positive terminal
> negative terminal
> potential difference
> voltage
> voltmeter
> origin
> thermistor
> sensor
> diode
> light dependent resistor (LDR)

Resistors and Energy Transfers

You must be able to:

- Calculate the resistance of two or more resistors in series or in parallel
- Understand that resistors transfer energy out of circuits by heating and motors are used to transfer energy out of circuits by doing work
- Recall that rate of transfer of energy is power
- Perform calculations on power, energy, voltage, current and time for use of electricity by appliances at home.

Resistors in Series

- Resistors can be connected in **series** – one after the other.
- Since both resistors resist current, their total resistance is greater than their individual resistance.
- Total resistance is the sum of the individual resistances:

total resistance (R_t) = resistance 1 (R_1) + resistance 2 (R_2)

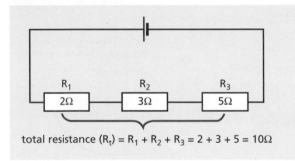

total resistance (R_t) = $R_1 + R_2 + R_3 = 2 + 3 + 5 = 10\Omega$

- The current in each of the resistors must be the same.
- Current is flow and, if there is only one route for it to flow along, it must be the same at all points.

potential difference (V) = current (A) × resistance (Ω)

- If the current is the same in two resistors but the resistances are different, the voltages must be different.
- The relative size of the voltages is the same as the relative size of the resistances.

$$\frac{\text{voltage 1 } (V_1)}{\text{voltage 2 } (V_2)} = \frac{\text{resistance 1 } (R_1)}{\text{resistance 2 } (R_2)}$$

Resistors in Parallel

- Resistors can be connected in **parallel** – one alongside the other.
- This gives current two routes to follow, so the total resistance is smaller than either of the resistors:

$$\frac{1}{\text{total resistance } (R_t)} = \frac{1}{\text{resistance 1} (R_1)} + \frac{1}{\text{resistance 2} (R_2)}$$

> **Key Point**
>
> When two resistors are in series, current must pass through both of them.

- Resistors in parallel have the same voltage.
- If the resistances of two resistors in parallel are different:
  - they do not carry the same current
  - the current will be larger in the smaller resistor.

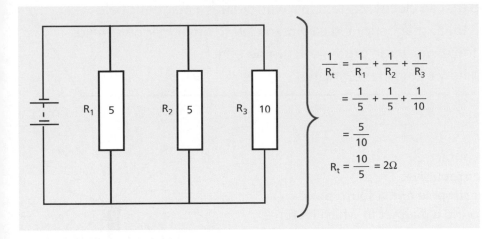

Key Point

When two resistors are in parallel, some of the current will go through one resistor and the rest through the other.

Transfer of Energy

- Current in resistors heats them. Thermal energy is transferred.
- Motors also transfer energy. They do that by exerting force that can make objects move – they do work.
- Motors are not designed to provide heat, but they do transfer some energy by heating their surroundings.

Electrical Power

- The rate at which a component in a circuit transfers energy is its power, measured in watts (W) or kilowatts (kW).
- Since power is rate of transfer of energy:

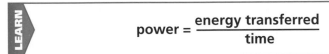

$$\text{power} = \frac{\text{energy transferred}}{\text{time}}$$

- Energy can be measured in joules (J), kilojoules (kJ) and kilowatt-hours (kWh).
- In circuits, power is related to current and voltage:

$$\text{power (W)} = \text{potential difference (V)} \times \text{current (A)}$$
$$= (\text{current (A)})^2 \times \text{resistance } (\Omega)$$

Key Point

One watt (W) and one joule (J) are small. So kW (1000 W) are often used for power of domestic appliances. The kilowatt-hour (kWh) is then used for measuring energy. A kilowatt-hour is the energy transferred in 1 hour by an appliance with a power of 1kW.

Quick Test

1. Calculate the total resistance of a 2Ω resistor and a 4Ω resistor when they are connected **a)** in series and **b)** in parallel.
2. Describe how motors transfer energy out of a circuit.
3. A resistor has a current of 1.5A and a potential difference of 12V.
   a) Calculate how much heat energy it transfers to its surroundings in 60 seconds.
   b) What is the power of the resistor?

Magnetic Fields and Motors

You must be able to:

- Relate diagrams of magnetic field lines to possible forces
- Recall that strong electromagnets can be made from coils of wire
- Understand that an electric current in a wire creates a magnetic field
- HT Understand that a magnetic field can interact with other magnetic fields to create a force, which can produce a turning effect
- HT Understand how a loudspeaker works.

Magnetic Fields

- Magnets can exert force without contact.
- Magnetic force can be attractive or repulsive.
- Every magnet has two poles – a north pole and a south pole.
- The **magnetic field** is the space around a magnet in which its force can act.
- **Magnetic field lines** are used in diagrams to represent direction of force that would act on a small north pole at different places in a magnetic field.
- The distances between magnetic field lines show the strength of

  the magnetic field at different places.

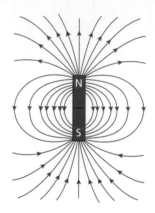

HT **Magnetic flux density** is a measure of the strength of a magnetic field at a specific point in the field.
HT The unit of magnetic flux density is the tesla (T).

Permanent and Induced Magnets

- Some iron and steel objects are **permanent magnets**.
- Others become magnetic when they are in a magnetic field – that kind of magnetism is called **induced magnetism**.

The Earth's Magnetic Field

- The Earth has a magnetic field, as if there is a huge magnet inside.
- Compass needles line up along magnetic field lines if they are free to do so.
- A compass needle that can move up and down as well as round and round dips towards or away from the ground.
- These compasses show that in most places the Earth's magnetic field is not parallel to the ground.

Magnetic Field Due to an Electric Current

- Wires with electric current have a magnetic field.
- The strength of the magnetic field at a point around a wire with current depends on the size of the current and also on the distance from the wire.
- A coil of wire with an iron core can be a strong **electromagnet**.
- This can also be called a **solenoid**.

A Solenoid

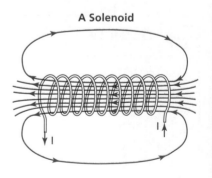

HT Magnetic Force on a Wire

- A conductor (such as a wire) with an electric current experiences a force when it is in a magnetic field.
- The relative directions of the current, the magnetic field lines and the force on the conductor can be predicted using **Fleming's left-hand rule**.

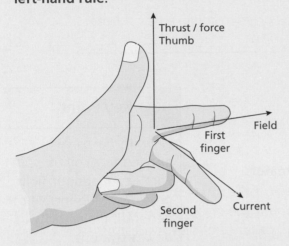

Thrust / force
Thumb

Field

First finger

Second finger

Current

- The force depends on the magnetic flux density, the current and the length of the conductor in the field:

> **force on a conductor (at right-angles to a magnetic field) carrying a current (N) = magnetic field strength (T) × current (A) × length (m)**

- Pairs of forces on a coil of wire can produce rotation – this is how **motors** work.

Forces on a coil carrying an electric current in a magnetic field produce a turning effect.

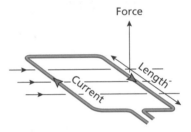

Force

Length

Current

HT Loudspeakers

- The basic principle of **loudspeakers** is the same as for motors:
  - An alternating current in a coil creates an alternating magnetic field that interacts with the field of a permanent magnet.
  - The interaction produces force and, therefore, motion.
- The current in a loudspeaker changes, with a pattern that matches the original sound.
- The pattern changes rapidly, so the force and the motion change rapidly, to produce vibrations and, therefore, sound.

Key Words

magnetic field
magnetic field lines
HT magnetic flux density
permanent magnetism
induced magnetism
electromagnet
solenoid
HT Fleming's left-hand rule
HT motor
HT loudspeaker

> ### Quick Test
>
> 1. Sketch the magnetic field pattern around a bar magnet and use it to show areas where the field is strong and weak.
> 2. Describe the similarities and differences between the magnetic field around a solenoid and the magnetic field around a permanent bar magnet.
> 3. HT Explain what causes the forces on the coil of a motor.

Electromagnetism

You must be able to:

- **HT** Understand that when a wire is forced through a magnetic field, or is in a changing magnetic field, a voltage is induced in it and the voltage can make a current flow if the wire is part of a circuit
- **HT** Understand how a microphone creates an electrical signal from vibrations
- Understand the principle of a transformer
- **HT** Understand why the number of turns on each coil in a transformer is important.

HT Inducing Voltage

- If a conductor is in a changing magnetic field, a voltage or potential difference is created. This is an **induced voltage**.
- Induced voltage can be used to generate electricity in **alternators**, **dynamos**, **microphones** and **transformers**.
- The direction of the voltage acts to oppose the changing magnetic field.

HT Alternators

- An alternator is a device with a coil of wire that must be turned by external forces.
- The coil lies in a changing magnetic field, due to its motion, so a voltage is induced in the coil.
- The direction of the current produced creates a magnetic field and gives rise to a force that opposes the rotation of the coil, so energy must be continuously supplied to the coil to keep it turning.
- The coil transfers energy to its circuit from the external source that makes it rotate.
- An alternator produces **alternating current, a.c.**
- Alternating current repeatedly changes direction.

HT Dynamos

- A dynamo uses the same principle, but connections to the dynamo mean that the current is always in the same direction.
- It provides **direct current, d.c.**

HT Microphones

- A microphone uses vibration of a conductor in a magnetic field to induce a matching pattern of voltage.
- That allows sounds to be transmitted, **amplified** and recorded in electrical systems.
- A microphone generates small voltages that vary in a pattern that copies the pattern of sound.

HT Key Point

An external force applied to a coil of wire in a magnetic field provides the principle of generating electricity in power stations.

Alterating Current, a.c.

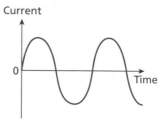

Constant Direct Current, d.c.

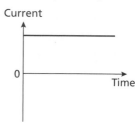

Varying Direct Current, d.c.

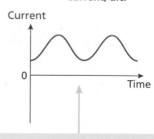

The direction doesn't change.

Transformers

- Alternating current in a coil produces a changing magnetic field.
- The changing magnetic field can induce voltage in a second coil, so energy can transfer from a coil in one circuit to a coil in another.
- A transformer is a device that does this.
- The coil with the applied a.c. (alternating current) and changing magnetic field is the primary coil.
- The coil in which a voltage is induced is the secondary coil.

HT The size of the voltage in each of the two coils is related to the number of turns.

HT In an ideal transformer:

$$\frac{\text{potential difference across primary coil (V)}}{\text{potential difference across secondary coil (V)}} = \frac{\text{number of turns in primary coil}}{\text{number of turns in secondary coil}}$$

HT In an ideal transformer that transfers all of the energy that it receives (from the primary circuit to the secondary circuit):

> **potential difference across primary coil (V) × current in primary coil (A) = potential difference across secondary coil (V) × current in secondary coil (A)**

HT In reality, some energy is lost, and dissipates, from transformers.

- A **step-up transformer** has a bigger voltage in the secondary coil than in the primary coil.
- A **step-down transformer** has a bigger voltage in the primary coil than in the secondary coil.
- A transformer cannot create energy (in fact, it loses some energy to its surroundings due to heating).
- When voltage steps up, current must decrease, and when voltage steps down, current must increase.

A Step-Up Transformer

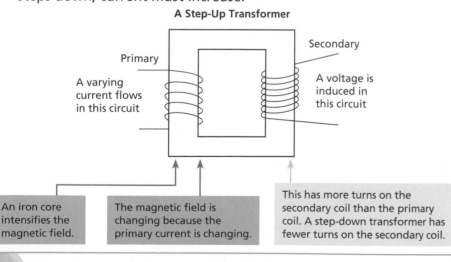

Primary

Secondary

A varying current flows in this circuit

A voltage is induced in this circuit

An iron core intensifies the magnetic field.

The magnetic field is changing because the primary current is changing.

This has more turns on the secondary coil than the primary coil. A step-down transformer has fewer turns on the secondary coil.

Key Point

Transformers transfer energy from one circuit to another, without any electrical contact between the circuits.

Key Point

A transformer only works with applied a.c., not with d.c. The output at the secondary coil is also a.c.

Key Words

HT **induced voltage**
HT **alternator**
HT **dynamo**
HT **microphone**
transformer
HT **alternating current (a.c.)**
HT **direct current (d.c.)**
HT **amplify**
step-up transformer
step-down transformer

Quick Test

1. HT Outline the principles an alternator uses.
2. Outline the principles a transformer uses.

Review Questions

Matter, Models and Density

1 What is the unit of density?

    A kgm   **C** kg/m²

    B kg/m   **D** kg/m³   [1]

2 Which of these models of an atom is not normally used now?   [1]

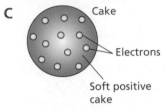

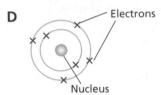

3 Which of the following best describes the nuclear model of the atom?

    A the radius of the nucleus is much smaller than the radius of the atom

    B the radius of the nucleus is the same as the radius of the atom

    C the radius of the nucleus is much bigger than the radius of the atom   [1]

4 Which of the following do atoms contain?

    A very small positively charged electrons

    B very small negatively charged electrons

    C small negatively charged protons

    D small positively charged neutrons.   [1]

5 What is the density of material in space?

    A zero   **C** the same as on Earth

    B a little less than on Earth, but not zero   **D** more than on Earth   [1]

6 Ernest Rutherford made a discovery that led to the development of a new model of the atom.

    Explain what happened in his experiment and what he concluded from it.   [4]

7 a) Calculate the density of a material if 1.0kg has a volume of 0.002m³. [3]

HT b) Will the material in part a) float in water? [1]
You must give a reason for your answer.

8 Explain the differences between:

a) an atom and a nucleus [2]

b) an atom and an ion [2]

c) an electron and a proton [2]

d) a proton and a neutron. [2]

Total Marks _____ / 21

Temperature and State

1 Which of these does **not** change during a change of state?

A density   B energy   C mass   D volume   [1]

2 In a gas, what does molecular bombardment cause?

A melting   B freezing   C energy   D pressure   [1]

3 Which of the following describes a change in state?

A reversible   B irreversible   C chemical   [1]

4 Complete the following sentence.

The specific heat capacity of a material is used for prediction involving:

A change in temperature and changes of state that require (take in) energy.

B change in temperature and any change of state.

C change of state only.

D change in temperature only. [1]

5 Which has most internal energy?

    A an ice cube of mass 0.01kg and a temperature of −1°C

    B a pan of water with mass 0.5kg and a temperature of 80°C

    C a lake of water with mass 1×10^7kg and a temperature of 8°C

    D a cloud of steam with mass 5kg and a temperature of 100°C   [1]

6 Snow can melt slowly, even when the temperature is a few degrees above freezing point. Why is this?

    A its specific heat capacity is large   **C** energy is needed to melt it

    B its specific heat capacity is small   **D** it gives out energy as it melts   [1]

> Total Marks .... / 6

Pressure

1 HT Which of these does **not** affect the pressure acting on a body that is immersed in liquid?

    A the density of the body   **C** gravitational field strength

    B the density of the liquid   [1]

2 How does a gas exert pressure on surfaces?   [2]

3 What is the general relationship between atmospheric pressure and height above the Earth's surface?   [1]

4 HT The pressure at a point inside a liquid = density of liquid × depth × g
The density of water is 1000kg/m³.

    a) Calculate the pressure due to water, in pascals (Pa), experienced by a diver at a depth of 15m.   [2]

    b) The total pressure on the diver = pressure due to the water + atmospheric pressure.

        If atmospheric pressure is 100 000Pa, what is the total pressure?   [2]

    c) By what factor is the total pressure on the diver at 15m depth greater than pressure when standing on the ground?   [2]

> Total Marks .... / 10

Journeys

1 What is 100 miles in kilometres?

$$\frac{1 \text{ mile}}{1 \text{ kilometre}} = \frac{8}{5}$$

A 160km **B** 62.5km **C** 60km **D** 21.6km [1]

2 How far can you walk in 2.5 hours at an average speed of 1m/s?

A 1440m **B** 9000m **C** 10 800m **D** 12 600m [1]

3 Which of these is the fastest speed?

$$\frac{1 \text{ mile}}{1 \text{ kilometre}} = \frac{8}{5}$$

A 36km/h **C** 10m/s

B 36 000m/h **D** 25mph [1]

4 Which graph shows constant velocity?

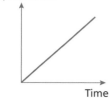

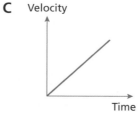

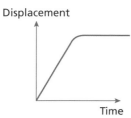

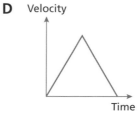

[1]

5 A car is travelling at 5m/s and then speeds up to 15m/s. It takes 10s to do this.

What is the car's acceleration?

A 0.5m/s² **B** 1m/s² **C** 2m/s² **D** 10m/s² [1]

Review Questions

6   The diagram shows the velocity vectors of a car at two times, T_1 and T_2, one minute apart.

T_1 T_2

a) What has happened to the speed of the car?   [1]

b) What has happened to the velocity of the car?   [1]

c) Has the car accelerated or decelerated?   [1]

d) What can you say about the force acting on the car?   [1]

7   a) A sports car can accelerate from standstill (velocity = 0) to 30m/s in 10s.

    What is its acceleration?   [3]

    b) If the mass of the car is 1000kg, what is its kinetic energy:

        i)   when it is standing still?   [1]

        ii) when it is moving at 30m/s?   [3]

    c) What average force is needed to accelerate the car?   [3]

    d) Use the following equation
        (final velocity (m/s))² – (initial velocity (m/s))² = 2 × acceleration (m/s²) × distance (m)
        to work out the distance the car travels during this acceleration.   [2]

    e) Calculate the amount of work that is needed for the car's acceleration.   [3]

    f) What is the power at which the car gains energy?   [2]

Total Marks _____ / 26

Forces

1 What type of force acts on the Earth to keep it in orbit?

   A electric or electrostatic force   **C** magnetic force

   B gravitational force   **D** resistive force   [1]

2 Which of these always causes acceleration?

   A unbalanced or net force   **C** constant velocity

   B balanced forces   **D** constant pressure   [1]

3 How much force is needed to accelerate a mass of 20kg by 4m/s²?

   A 5N   **B** 16N   **C** 24N   **D** 80N   [1]

4 **a)** When a person steps off a boat, what does their foot do to the boat?   [1]

   b) What happens to the boat:

      i) if it is much more massive than the person?   [1]

      ii) if it is not much more massive than the person?   [1]

   c) Sketch the forces acting on the person and on the boat.   [3]

5 Humans cannot jump very high.

   Why not?   [1]

6 Describe the net force or resultant force for each of the following examples.

   a)   [1]

   b)   [1]

   c)   [1]

Total Marks .... / 13

Review Questions

Force, Energy and Power

1 What is power the same as?

    A change of momentum   **C** rate of energy transfer

    B kinetic energy   **D** strength   [1]

2 A person has to do work to push a cupboard across a room.

    a) If they push it for 2.5m with an average force of 180N, how much work do they do?   [3]

    b) If the cupboard is floating in space, and it experiences a force of 180N over a distance of 2.5m, how much kinetic energy does it gain?   [1]

    c) Why doesn't the cupboard in the room gain kinetic energy?   [1]

    d) On Earth, imagine that the cupboard experiences an **upwards** force equal to its weight, 300N, and rises steadily to a height of 2.5m.

       What can you say about the cupboard's energy?   [3]

Total Marks _____ / 9

Changes of Shape

1 Which of the following best describes the relationship between force and extension for an elastic spring?

    A constant   **B** linear   **C** non-linear   **D** varying   [1]

2 **a)** What is the weight on Earth, in newtons (N), of a ball with mass of 1.2kg?   [3]

    b) If g_{moon} and $g_{jupiter}$ are 1.6N/kg and 25N/kg, how much will the ball weigh on **i)** the Moon and **ii)** on Jupiter?   [2]

Total Marks _____ / 6

Levers, Gears and Hydraulic Systems

1 Complete the sentence.

A lever is a force multiplier. This means that:

A the applied force is bigger than the load force and moves further.

B the applied force is bigger than the load force and doesn't move so far.

C the load force is bigger than the applied force and moves further.

D the load force is bigger than the applied force and doesn't move so far. [1]

2 Which of these diagrams accurately shows a lever being used to lift a load? [1]

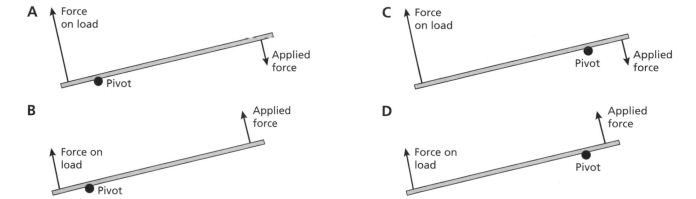

3 A force of 180N is made to act on a movable piston of a hydraulic system.
The area of the piston is 0.2m².
The system has a second moveable piston with an area of 0.8m².

a) What is the pressure inside the system? [3]

b) How much force acts at the second piston? [3]

c) What is the use of a hydraulic system like this? [1]

4 A child with weight 30kg sits 1.5m from the pivot of a seesaw.

Calculate where another child should sit to balance the seesaw, if she has a weight of 20kg. [3]

Total Marks _____ / 12

Practice Questions

Electric Charge

1 What must a body have to experience an electric force?

    A positive charge   **C** either positive or negative charge

    B negative charge   **D** positive and negative charge   **[1]**

2 Why can an object, such as a balloon, become charged when rubbed?

    A friction creates electrons

    B friction destroys electrons

    C friction transfers electrons

    D friction gives electrons extra charge   **[1]**

3 What is produced by the movement of many electrons in the same direction?

    A an electric charge   **B** an electric current   **C** an electric resistance   **[1]**

4 What is the unit of resistance?

    A amp   **B** coulomb   **C** ohm   **D** volt   **[1]**

5 Electric force can be attractive or repulsive.

    a) What does that tell us about electric charge?   **[1]**

    b) Sketch two charged bodies attracting each other and show their charge.   **[1]**

    c) Sketch two charged bodies repelling each other and show their charge.   **[1]**

6 Explain why:

    a) metals are good at conducting electricity   **[1]**

    b) a resistor gets hot when the current is large   **[2]**

    c) resistance is smaller when two resistors are in parallel than when there is only one of them.   **[1]**

Total Marks _____ / 11

Circuits

1. What voltage is needed to drive a 2.5A current through a 20Ω resistor?

   A 8V   B 20V   C 22.5V   D 50V   [1]

2. Which of these statements is correct?

   A The relationship between current and voltage in a wire is always linear.

   B The relationship between current and voltage in a wire is linear provided the wire does not get hot.

   C The relationship between current and voltage in a wire is always non-linear.

   D The relationship between current and voltage in a wire is non-linear provided the wire does not get hot.   [1]

3. Which of these diagrams shows the correct connection of an ammeter and a voltmeter?   [1]

   A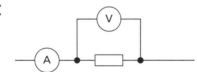

   B

   C

   D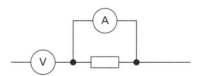

4. How does a resistor transfer energy to its surroundings?

   A heating   C storing energy

   B doing work   D creating energy   [1]

5. At what rate does a resistor transfer energy if it carries a current of 0.5A and is connected to a voltage of 1.5V?

   A 0.75W   B 1.0W   C 2.0W   D 3W   [1]

6 What is the SI unit of energy in electric circuits?

A amp **B** joule **C** volt **D** watt [1]

7 Which of these equations is **not** correct?

A charge moved = current × time

B potential difference = current × resistance

C energy transferred = power × time

D resistance = current × potential difference [1]

8 Explain the problem, if any, with each of these circuits.

a) [1]

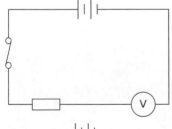

b) [1]

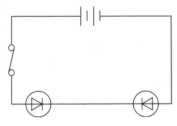

c) [1]

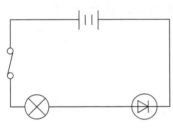

d) [1]

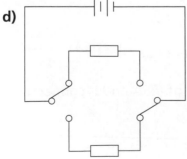

9 Explain what each of the following components are used for.

a) battery or cell [1]

b) ammeter [1]

c) voltmeter [1]

d) resistor [1]

e) diode [1]

f) thermistor [2]

g) LDR [2]

10 A current of 1.5A passes through a 6Ω resistor. Calculate:

a) the voltage [3]

b) the amount of charge that flows through the resistor in 60 seconds [3]

c) the energy transferred by the resistor in 60 seconds [3]

d) the rate of energy transfer. [3]

Total Marks _____ / 32

Resistors and Energy Transfers

1 Which of these circuits has the least resistance? (All of the resistors are identical.)

A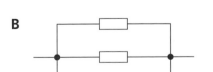

C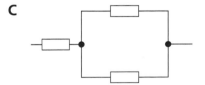

B

D [1]

Total Marks _____ / 1

Practice Questions

Magnetic Fields and Motors

1 Which of these is a correct diagram of a magnetic field pattern?

A
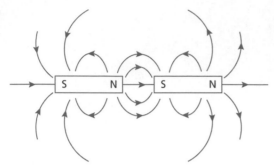

B
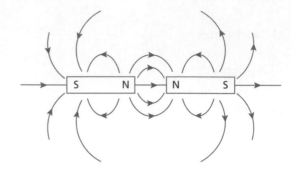

C
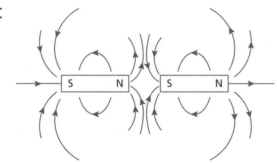

D
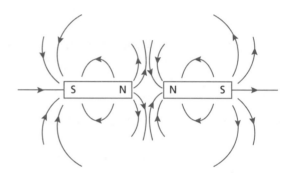

[1]

2 A compass is lying close to a coil of wire that is part of a circuit.

When does the compass needle move?

A when the current in the coil is constant

B only when the current in the coil is turned on

C only when the current in the coil is turned off

D when the current in the coil is turned on or off [1]

3 HT Why does a simple electric motor produce rotation?

    A the forces on opposite sides of a coil are in the same direction

    B the forces on opposite sides of a coil are in opposite directions

    C the current in the coil is constant

    D the current in the coil is changing [1]

4 HT A wire carrying a current is in a magnetic field.

Which of these graphs shows the correct relative orientations of electric current, magnetic field lines and force on the wire?

A

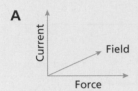

C

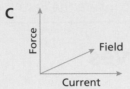

B

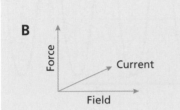

D

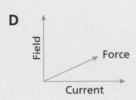

[1]

5 Complete the sentence.

A north pole of a magnet:

A attracts another north pole.

C repels a south pole.

B repels another north pole.

D attracts a north pole or a south pole. [1]

6 What does a magnetic field line show? [2]

7 How do we know that the Earth is magnetic? [1]

8 What happens to magnetic field strength as distance away from a magnet increases? [1]

Total Marks _____ / 9

Electromagnetism

1 HT What is the difference between a.c. and d.c.? [2]

2 HT How does a loudspeaker work? [6]

Total Marks _____ / 8

Sound, Sonar and Ultrasound

You must be able to:

- Recall that sound waves are longitudinal and travel from sources through substances (media)
- Describe absorption and reflection of sound and ultrasound
- **HT** Understand how our ears detect sound
- Understand amplitude, frequency and wavelength of waves
- **HT** Describe how waves from earthquakes show that that there is liquid deep inside the Earth.

Properties of Waves

- All waves have a:
  - **frequency** – the number of waves passing a fixed point per second, measured in hertz (Hz)
  - **amplitude** – the maximum displacement that any particle achieves from its undisturbed position in metres (m)
  - **wavelength** – the distance from one point on a wave to the equivalent point on the next wave in metres (m)
  - **period** – the time taken for one complete oscillation in seconds (s).

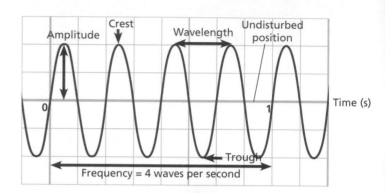

Travelling Vibrations

- Vibrations from a source pass into a nearby material or **medium** and travel through as **sound waves**.
- Sound waves travel more easily through solids and liquids than through gases.
- However, sound waves can reach our ears by travelling through air.
- Sound waves are **longitudinal waves** – the vibrations of the particles of the medium are parallel to the direction of travel of the waves.
- Higher frequency sounds have shorter wavelengths.
- High pitch sounds are related to high frequency vibration and low pitch or deep sounds are related to lower frequency vibration.

> **Key Point**
>
> 1Hz means one cycle of vibration per second.

> **Key Point**
>
> Sound is emitted by vibrating sources. In a sound wave, particles of the medium only vibrate. They do not travel from the source to our ears.

HT Hearing

- Sound waves make our eardrums vibrate.
- The vibration is amplified by small bones in our ears.
- The vibration passes into liquid in the cochlea in the **inner ear**.
- Very small hairs vibrate to create electrical changes that pass to the brain.
- We can hear sounds with frequencies as low as 20Hz, up to about 18 kilohertz (kHz). 1kHz = 1000Hz.

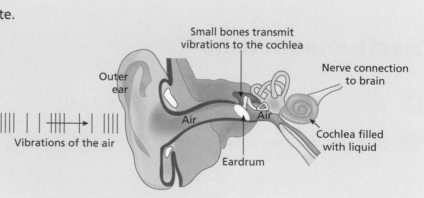

Reflection and Absorption of Sound

- Surfaces, especially hard surfaces, can reflect sound.
- Reflected sounds that are loud enough to hear clearly are called echoes.
- Surfaces, especially soft surfaces, **absorb** sound. The energy of vibration passes into the material.

Sonar and Ultrasound

- **Sonar** uses reflected sounds to detect objects and measure distance.
- It works under water, because water **transmits** sound well.
- The speed of sound in water is about 1500m/s.
- Sonar uses **pulses** of sound.
- The faster the reflected sound returns to the source, the closer the reflecting object is.
- **Ultrasound** is sound with a frequency that is too high for humans to hear.
- It is used to scan unborn babies.
- The mother's body transmits the waves and reflection happens at different surfaces, including the surface of the baby.

HT Seismic Waves

- Two kinds of **seismic wave** travel through the Earth from earthquakes:
  - **P-waves** are longitudinal, like sound waves.
  - **S-waves** are **transverse** – the direction of vibration of rock is at right-angles to the direction of travel of the wave.
- S-waves can only travel through solids.
- There are regions where S-waves from earthquakes are not detected. This tells us that there is liquid deep inside the Earth.

Direction of travel of the wave

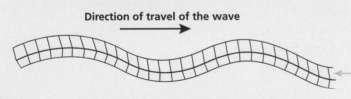

Direction of travel of the wave

Quick Test

1. State what all sources of sound do.
2. What property is unique to individual sound waves and allows us to distinguish between different sounds?
3. Describe the absorption of a wave.
4. What behaviours of sound do the techniques of sonar and ultrasound scanning make use of?
5. HT Explain how we know that the centre of the Earth is liquid.

Key Point

Sonar and ultrasound devices emit pulses and measure the time for the reflected waves to return. This provides information about distance to the reflecting surface.

HT Key Point

Waves that travel out from earthquakes – seismic waves – can be used to study the inside of the Earth.

P-waves are longitudinal. Blocks of rock are stretched and compressed (exaggerated here).

S-waves are transverse. Blocks of rock vibrate 'sideways' to the direction of travel of the wave.

Key Words

frequency
amplitude
wavelength
period
medium
sound wave
longitudinal wave
HT inner ear
absorb
sonar
transmit
pulse
ultrasound
HT seismic wave
HT P-wave
HT S-wave
HT transverse wave

Electromagnetic Radiation

You must be able to:

- Understand that vision is based on absorption of light in the eyes
- Use a ripple model of light to illustrate reflection and refraction
- Describe the electromagnetic spectrum, including sources, uses and hazards of different kinds of electromagnetic radiation
- Understand that high frequency radiation can ionise, and that ionisation can cause chemical changes in our bodies that can be harmful.

Light Waves

- Light travels as vibrations of electrical and magnetic fields – it is an **electromagnetic wave**.
- The vibrations are at right-angles to the direction of travel – light waves are **transverse waves**.
- Different frequencies or wavelengths of visible light have different effects on the cells in the **retinas** in our eyes.
- As a result, different electrical changes happen in our brains and we see different colours.
- Ripples on the surface of water are good models of transverse waves.
- These ripples can help to build a picture of light waves, i.e. water ripples are models of light waves.
- Ripples experience reflections at the edges of the water.
- When their speed changes, they experience **refraction**.
- When light travels from a source (an emitter of light):
  - no material travels
  - it transmits energy from the source to anything that absorbs it.
- When light is completely absorbed, it loses all of its energy and ceases to exist.

> **Key Point**
>
> Electromagnetic radiation transfers energy from the source to anything that absorbs it.

The Electromagnetic Spectrum

- The **electromagnetic spectrum** includes radio waves and **microwaves, infrared**, visible light, **ultraviolet (UV), X-rays** and **gamma rays**.
- These radiations all have the same speed in a vacuum.
- It is called the speed of light and is 300 000 000m/s or 3×10^8m/s.
- Radio waves have the longest wavelengths and the lowest frequency.
- X-rays and gamma rays have the shortest wavelength and the highest frequency.

> **LEARN**
>
> **wave speed (m/s) = frequency (Hz) × wavelength (m)**

The Electromagnetic Spectrum

Gamma rays X-rays Ultraviolet Visible light Infared Microwaves Radio waves

> **Key Point**
>
> Visible light is just a small range of radiations. It is part of a much bigger range, called the electromagnetic spectrum.

Using Different Kinds of Electromagnetic Radiation

- Radio and microwaves are used for communication – for sending signals between mobile phones, between radio stations and radio receivers (or 'radios'), and even to space probes far from Earth.
- Mobile phone networks use microwaves.
- Mobile phones emit and absorb (and so detect) microwaves.

> HT Radio and microwaves are emitted from electrical circuits with a rapidly varying current.
>
> HT The **oscillations** or vibrations of the current have the same frequency as the waves.
>
> HT All radio transmitters, including mobile phones, emit waves in this way.

- Microwaves with a frequency that water molecules are good at absorbing can be used to heat anything that contains water.
- Infrared radiation can cause heating.
- Infrared is emitted by all objects, and the higher their temperature the more energetic the radiation is.
- Infrared cameras can detect this, so they can detect objects that are warmer than their surroundings.
- Paint or ink that reflects UV radiation can be used to make marks on objects. The marks can only be seen using a UV light and UV detector.
- Bones absorb X-rays more strongly than the softer tissue, so shadow images of the human body can be produced, which clearly show bones and any other denser tissue.
- X-rays and gamma rays can be used to kill harmful organisms, such as bacteria.

Ionising Radiation

- X-rays and gamma rays **ionise** atoms strongly. Some UV can also ionise.
- When materials absorb energy from these radiations, the atoms have enough energy for electrons to escape from them.
- This can cause chemical changes in complicated molecules within our bodies, such as DNA, and lead to cancer. To avoid this, we must limit exposure to these radiations.
- For routine X-ray health checks, the benefits of the very low exposure to radiation outweigh the hazards.

> ## Key Point
>
> Radio waves are very useful for transmitting information. TV and radio broadcasting, mobile phones and Wi-Fi systems all use radio waves.

> ## Quick Test
>
> 1. Explain why ripples are better models of light waves than of sound waves.
> 2. What do all electromagnetic waves have in common?
> 3. List the parts of the electromagnetic spectrum in order of decreasing wavelength.
> 4. What happens to the frequency of electromagnetic waves as wavelength decreases?
> 5. Explain why some electromagnetic radiations cause ionisation, but others do not.

> ## Key Words
>
> electromagnetic wave
> transverse wave
> retina
> refraction
> electromagnetic spectrum
> microwave
> infrared
> ultraviolet (UV)
> X-ray
> gamma ray
> HT oscillation
> ionise

Waves at Surfaces and Inside Materials

You must be able to:

- Distinguish between reflection, refraction, transmission, absorption and scattering
- Understand that these processes usually depend on the frequency and wavelength of the radiation, and that this produces effects including colour
- Analyse reflection and refraction using ray diagrams
- Understand that refraction is due to change in speed of waves.

Reflection, Transmission, Absorption and Scattering

- Some materials are better at **reflecting** or **transmitting** waves, such as electromagnetic radiation, and others are better at **absorbing** them.
- Transmission and absorption happen inside materials.
- If the absorption is strong, the radiation does not penetrate far into the material.
- When **scattering** takes place inside a material, transmission becomes disturbed. The radiation spreads out in different directions.
- The amounts of transmission and absorption can depend on the frequency or wavelength of the radiation.

 For example, the atmosphere can transmit radio and visible radiations quite well over long distances, but absorbs ultraviolet (UV) radiation more strongly. This provides some protection from UV from the Sun.

- Reflection takes place at surfaces – at the interfaces or boundaries between materials.
- Objects that do not emit light are visible because they reflect light.

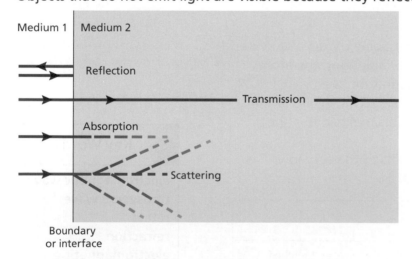

Differential Reflection and Absorption

- Red surfaces:
  - reflect red light (lower frequency, longer wavelength)
  - absorb other colours such as blue (higher frequency, shorter wavelength).
- This is **differential reflection** and **differential absorption**.
- Green surfaces reflect green light (mid-frequency, mid-wavelength) and absorb other colours.

> **Key Point**
>
> The reflection of light is very important to us. It allows us to see surfaces that do not emit their own light.

> **Key Point**
>
> Sometimes the amount of reflection depends on the frequency or wavelength of the light. Then a surface has a particular colour.

Differential Reflection at a Surface

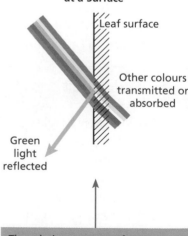

The relative amounts of transmission and absorption may depend on colour.

- Leaves are green because a substance inside them (chlorophyll) strongly absorbs red and blue light, but reflects green.

Reflection by Mirrors

- Mirrors have smooth surfaces so that reflection from them is easy to analyse and predict.
- **Rays**, and diagrams of rays, can be used to analyse and predict the direction of travel of light.
- A flat mirror is called a **plane** mirror.

Refraction

- **Refraction** takes place at surfaces – at **interfaces** or boundaries between materials that both transmit light (such as air and glass or water and glass).
- The transmitting materials are called media.
- Refraction happens when one medium is denser than the other, so the speed of the waves changes.
- Diagrams with normal lines and rays can be used to analyse and predict refraction.
- The angles in the two media are not the same.
- By forming glass into curved shapes, different refraction effects can be produced.

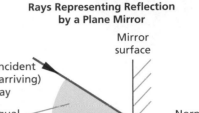

Rays Representing Reflection by a Plane Mirror

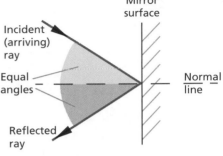

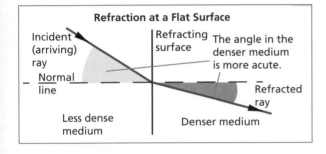

Refraction at a Flat Surface

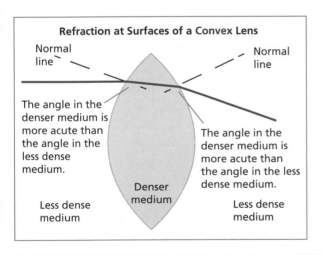

Refraction at Surfaces of a Convex Lens

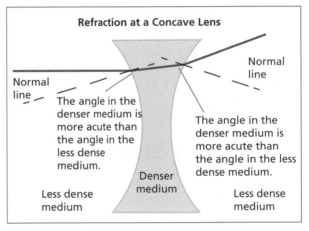

Refraction at a Concave Lens

> ## Key Point
>
> When a smooth surface reflects light, the angles either side of a normal line (a line at right-angles to the surface) are equal.

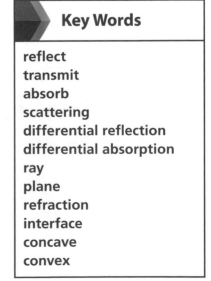

Key Words

reflect
transmit
absorb
scattering
differential reflection
differential absorption
ray
plane
refraction
interface
concave
convex

Quick Test

1. What is the difference between transmission and absorption?
2. State what happens to light waves that are completely absorbed.
3. Outline the difference between reflection and refraction.
4. Explain why reflection is important in how we see the world.

Nuclei of Atoms

You must be able to:

- Recall that nuclei have protons and neutrons, and that neutrons have no charge but protons have positive charge
- Use the form $^A_Z X$ to show different nuclear structures and isotopes
- Understand that most nuclei are stable, but some are unstable and can change by emission of particles and energy
- Distinguish between alpha, beta and gamma radiations.

Atoms, Nuclei and Ions

- The nuclei of atoms are very dense and positively charged.
- Electrons, with negative charge, orbit the nuclei in shells.
- The shells of electrons are different distances from nuclei.
- An electron in an atom can gain energy from electromagnetic radiation and move further away from the nucleus.
- When an electron moves closer to the nucleus the atom emits electromagnetic radiation.
- If an atom loses one of its outer electrons it becomes an ion – it is no longer electrically neutral but has overall positive charge.
- Nuclei contain protons and neutrons.
- The protons have the positive charge.
- Neutrons do not have electric charge – they are neutral.

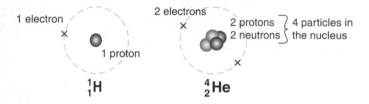

Atoms of Different Sizes

- Hydrogen atoms are the smallest atoms and have just one proton and one electron. Some hydrogen atoms can have one or even two neutrons in the nucleus.
- Iron atoms have 26 protons and 26 electrons. They can have 28, 30, 31 or 32 neutrons.
- Forms of the same element, with the same number of protons but different numbers of neutrons, are **isotopes**.
- The number of neutrons affects the mass of an atom, but does not affect the charge.

Stable and Unstable Nuclei

- Most of the nuclei in the world around us change very rarely – they are stable.
- But some can change, by emitting particles or radiation – they are unstable.
- These changes are called **radioactive emission** or **radioactive decay**.

> ### Key Point
>
> Protons and neutrons are approximately the same size but electrons are much smaller.

Absorption of Electromagnetic Radiation by an Atom

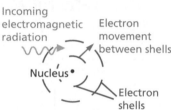

The electron gains energy and moves to a higher shell.

Emission of Electromagnetic Radiation by an Atom

The electron loses energy and falls to a lower shell.

Isotopes of Iron			
$^{54}_{26}$Fe	$^{56}_{26}$Fe	$^{57}_{26}$Fe	$^{58}_{26}$Fe

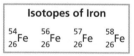

> ### Key Point
>
> Most of the nuclei of the atoms in your body are stable. They will not change by radioactive decay. A very small proportion of your atoms have unstable nuclei. Your body is a little radioactive. That's normal and natural.

Alpha Emission

- In one kind of emission, two protons and two neutrons leave the nucleus.
- They come out together, and we call the group of four an alpha particle. A continuous flow of alpha particles is **alpha radiation**.
- The alpha particles have enough energy to knock electrons out of atoms as they travel from the material into other materials. This is ionisation.

Decay, Fission and Fusion

You must be able to:

- Distinguish between irradiation and contamination
- HT Calculate the proportion of nuclei that are still undecayed after a given number of half-lives
- Describe nuclear fission and its use in nuclear power stations
- Describe the process of nuclear fusion.

Random Change and Half-Life

- A sample of radioactive material contains a very large number of atoms, so it contains a very large number of nuclei.
- The change or decay of a particular nucleus is unpredictable. It can be described as **random**.
- However, in very **unstable** materials the nuclei will change more quickly than the nuclei in more **stable** materials.
- In a sample of material, the number of nuclei that have not yet decayed decreases as, one by one, the nuclei decay.
- This follows a particular pattern – a **decay curve**.
- For a radioactive material, the time taken for the number of undecayed nuclei to reduce by half is always the same, no matter how many nuclei there are to start with.
- This time is called the **half-life** of the material.
- In a material with very unstable nuclei, the half-life is short.

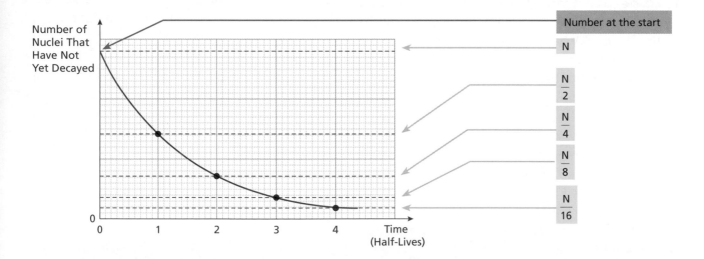

Half-Life and Hazards

- Materials with a long half-life can be a problem. They are not such strong sources of radiation moment by moment, but can remain radioactive for a long time.
- Materials with a short half-life can be very **hazardous** while their activity lasts, because they emit radiation at a high rate.
- If radioactive material becomes mixed up with other substances, the substances are **contaminated**. The mixture is radioactive.

Fission of Large Nuclei

- Some large unstable nuclei can change by splitting into two smaller nuclei.
- When they do this some neutrons are usually emitted.
- This is called **nuclear fission.**
- The two smaller nuclei and the neutrons usually fly apart with high energy. They pass energy to surrounding material, which heats it.
- In a substance such as uranium, fission can be encouraged by bombarding it with neutrons.
- When fission takes place, the neutrons that are emitted can make other nuclei split. This sets off a **chain reaction**.
- Nuclear power stations use energy from nuclear fission to heat water to make steam. The steam turns turbines.
- The smaller nuclei that are made by fission in power stations are usually radioactive or unstable. They are waste products of the power stations.
- Storing these radioactive substances safely is a big problem, especially since some have long half-lives and will be hazardous for a very long time.

Fusion of Small Nuclei

- **Nuclear fusion** is another change to nuclei, but very different.
- In fusion, small nuclei join together. This can also pass energy into surrounding material.
- There are no nuclear fusion power stations yet, because it is a very difficult process to control.
- This is unfortunate, because nuclear fusion does not have the same problems with waste materials as nuclear fission does.

> **Key Point**
>
> The Sun's source of energy is nuclear fusion.

> **Key Point**
>
> Nuclear fusion is the joining together of small nuclei. The process releases energy. In both fission and fusion, the energy transferred comes from a small reduction in mass of the particles.

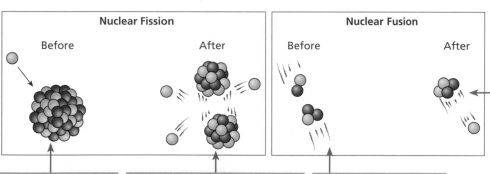

Nuclear Fission

Before   After

Nuclear Fusion

Before   After

...they can join together.

Some large nuclei can absorb (take in) an extra neutron. it makes them unstable.

They split into two smaller nuclei and some free neutrons. These particles fly apart at high speed – they carry a lot of energy.

If some small nuclei get close enough together…

Key Words

random
unstable
stable
decay curve
half-life
hazardous
contaminated
nuclear fission
chain reaction
nuclear fusion

Quick Test

1. Outline the main difference between nuclear fission and fusion.
2. Explain why materials with a short half-life are a hazard.
3. Explain why materials with a long half-life are a hazard.
4. Explain why contamination with radioactive material is a problem.
5. **HT** If there are N nuclei in a sample of a single radioactive material, how many will there be after **three** half-lives?

Review Questions

Electric Charge

1 Between which of these pairs of particles will there be a force of attraction?

A (+)   (+)

B Neutral ○   (+)

C Neutral ○   (−)

D (+)   (−) [1]

2 Inside atoms, which particles have electric charge?

A neutrons

B neutrons and protons

C neutrons, protons and electrons

D protons and electrons [1]

3 Why is it difficult to give a static charge to a metal object?

A electrons can easily flow on and off the object

B protons can easily flow on and off the object

C there are no electrons in metals

D electrons in metals can't move [1]

4 What does the movement of many electrons in the same direction produce?

A an electric charge

B an electric current

C an electric resistance [1]

5 Which of these is a correct diagram of electric field lines?

A
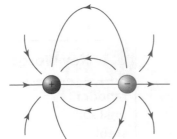

B
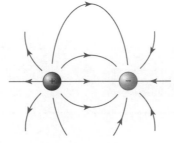

C
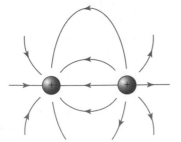

D
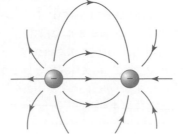

[1]

6 What is the unit of charge?

A amp

B coulomb

C joule

D volt   [1]

7 Which of these is a correct equation?

A current = charge × time

B current = $\dfrac{charge}{time}$

C charge = $\dfrac{current}{time}$

D time = current × charge   [1]

Total Marks _____ / 7

Circuits

1 What component is this the symbol for?

                                                                           [1]

2 Which of these will increase the current in a circuit?

A increasing voltage and keeping resistance the same

B increasing resistance and keeping voltage the same

C decreasing voltage and keeping resistance the same

D decreasing voltage and increasing resistance   [1]

Review Questions

3 Explain:

a) the difference between a volt (V) and a kilovolt (kV) [1]

b) the difference between a cell and a battery [1]

c) the difference between series and parallel connections [1]

d) the difference between an ammeter and a voltmeter [1]

e) the different ways in which ammeters and voltmeters are connected into circuits to investigate the current–voltage relationship for a component, such as a diode. [1]

4 a) Draw a circuit diagram for a circuit you would use to investigate the relationship between current and voltage for a filament lamp. [5]

b) A filament lamp contains a wire that gets hot.

Sketch a current–voltage graph for a filament lamp. [4]

c) Explain why the graph in part **b)** is not perfectly straight. [2]

Total Marks _____ / 18

Resistors and Energy Transfers

1 Which of these pairs are both units of energy?

A volt and joule

B watt and joule

C watt and kilowatt

D joule and kilowatt-hour [1]

2 What happens to:

a) the resistance of a thermistor when its temperature increases? [1]

b) the resistance of an LDR when light level decreases? [1]

3 A kettle is rated at 2.0kW.

a) Of what physical quantity is kW a unit? [1]

b) During 1 week, the kettle is used for a total of 2.5 hours.

How much energy does it transfer in the week? Give your answer in kWh. [3]

c) The hour and the kWh are not SI units.

What are the SI units for the same physical quantities? [2]

d) Why are SI units not always used when working with appliances like kettles? [1]

e) Repeat the calculation from part b), this time using SI units. [2]

Total Marks _____ / 12

Magnetic Fields and Motors

1 HT What information does magnetic flux density provide?

   A the size of the current in a coil

   B the size of the current in a magnet

   C the strength of magnetic field

   D the size of magnetic field [1]

2 HT What is the unit of magnetic flux density?

   A amp   C tesla

   B ohm   D volt [1]

3 Describe how you can show that a coil of wire carrying an electric current has a magnetic field around it. [2]

4 A solenoid is a useful electromagnet.

How can you increase the magnetic effect in the space around the coil? [3]

Review Questions

5 HT How much force acts on a wire of length 0.15m that carries a current of 2.5A in a magnetic field of flux density 0.12T?

force on a conductor (at right-angles to a magnetic field) carrying a current =
magnetic flux density × current × length [2]

6 HT In d.c. motors, the force on each side of the coil would not reverse and would not produce continuing rotation without a special connection to the power supply.

Explain this problem. [6]

Total Marks _____ / 15

Electromagnetism

1 HT When is a potential difference induced in a wire?

A when it is in a positive magnetic field

B when it is in a negative magnetic field

C when it is in a constant magnetic field

D when it is in a changing magnetic field [1]

2 HT Which device generates a direct current (d.c.)?

A an alternator   C a motor

B a dynamo   D a transformer [1]

3 HT What does a step-up transformer do?

A increase current   C increase power

B increase energy   D increase voltage [1]

4 HT Which of the following best describes alternators and dynamos?

    A   motion of the coil produces a magnetic force that opposes the motion

    B   motion of the coil produces a magnetic force that helps the motion

    C   motion of the coil produces a magnetic force that alternately helps and opposes the motion

    D   motion of the coil produces a magnetic force that does not affect the motion   **[1]**

5 HT What happens in a microphone?

    A   voltage is induced by relative motion of a conductor and a magnetic field

    B   voltage is induced due to changing current in a coil

    C   voltage is induced due to changing resistance of a wire

    D   voltage is induced directly by air pressure   **[1]**

6 HT A transformer has 240 turns on its primary coil and 24 turns on its secondary coil.

    a)   What is the purpose of the primary coil?   **[1]**

    b)   What happens in the secondary coil?   **[1]**

    c)   Is this a step-up or step-down transformer?   **[1]**

    d)   If a voltage of 240V is applied to the primary coil, what will be the size of the voltage in the secondary coil if there are no energy losses?   **[1]**

7 HT An ordinary loudspeaker has a coil of wire.

    a)   In what way does the current in the coil vary?   **[1]**

    b)   How does this produce sound?   **[2]**

Total Marks _____ / 12

Practice Questions

Sound, Sonar and Ultrasound

1 What term is given to the number of vibrations per second?

    A amplitude   **B** frequency   **C** speed   **D** wavelength [1]

2 If ripples on water have a wavelength of 0.1m and a frequency of 5Hz, what is their speed?

    A 0.5m/s   **B** 1.0m/s   **C** 1.5m/s   **D** 50m/s [1]

3 Which of these statements is **true**?

    A Only transverse waves carry energy.

    B Only longitudinal waves carry energy.

    C Transverse and longitudinal waves carry energy.

    D Neither transverse nor longitudinal waves carry energy. [1]

4 Sonar is a method of using sounds waves to detect objects under water, and their distance away.

  Which effect does this most rely on?

    A absorption   **B** transmission   **C** reflection   **D** refraction [1]

5 How does your voice make sound?

    A by absorbing   **B** by transmitting   **C** by refracting   **D** by vibrating [1]

6 HT Which of these sound frequencies can humans hear?

    A 5Hz   **C** 50 000Hz

    B 500Hz   **D** 50 000 000Hz [1]

7 What does a source of waves do?

    A absorbs waves   **C** reflects waves

    B emits waves   **D** transmits waves [1]

8 Which of the following is another word for 'range'?

    A amplitude   **C** spectrum

    B speed   **D** wavelength [1]

9 HT Which of these statements about seismic waves is **true**?

    A P-waves are longitudinal and S-waves are transverse.

    B P-waves are transverse and S-waves are longitudinal.

    C P-waves and S-waves are longitudinal.

    D P-waves and S-waves are transverse. [1]

10 HT Which of the following does not happen to seismic waves as they pass through the Earth?

    A absorption   **B** reflection   **C** refraction   **D** detection [1]

11 Which of these is the name given to technology that uses sound to explore under the sea and deep water?

    A Sonar   **B** Radar   **C** Laser   **D** Ultrasound [1]

12 HT Why is ultrasound a good technology to use for scanning unborn babies?

    A Ultrasound waves travel long distances.

    B Ultrasound waves are only weakly reflected.

    C Ultrasound waves provide warmth for the baby.

    D Ultrasound waves have very low hazard. [1]

Total Marks _____ / 12

Electromagnetic Radiation

1 Which of these have the longest wavelength?

    A radio waves   **C** visible light waves

    B ultraviolet waves   **D** X-rays [1]

2 Reflection of some frequencies of light but not others by different surfaces gives the surfaces:

    A brightness   **B** colour   **C** texture   **D** gloss [1]

3 Complete the sentence.

The colour that surfaces appear is due to different interactions with different:

A amplitudes of light.   C speeds of light.

B brightnesses of light.   D wavelengths of light.   [1]

4 The frequency of visible light travelling through glass is 4×10^{14}Hz and its wavelength is 5×10^{-7}m. What is its speed?   [3]

> **Total Marks** .... / 6

Waves at Surfaces and Inside Materials

1 When waves pass from one medium into another their speed usually changes.

What happens to frequency and wavelength?   [2]

2 Light can travel easily through a vacuum but it interacts with materials.

Name the interactions that happen:

a) at the surfaces of materials   [2]

b) inside materials.   [3]

3 Complete these ray diagrams of reflection and refraction at flat surfaces.

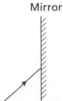   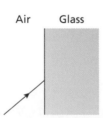

[3]

4 Complete these ray diagrams of reflection and refraction at curved surfaces.

   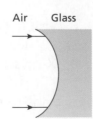

[3]

5 HT Which of the following best describes the Earth's atmosphere?

 A good at absorbing ultraviolet radiation and good at transmitting visible radiation

 B good at absorbing ultraviolet radiation and bad at transmitting visible radiation

 C bad at absorbing ultraviolet radiation and good at transmitting visible radiation

 D bad at absorbing ultraviolet radiation and bad at transmitting visible radiation [1]

6 HT The Earth receives energy from the Sun and also re-emits energy back into space.

 Which of the following best describes the re-emitted radiation?

 A higher speed than the radiation that arrives from the Sun

 B lower speed than the radiation that arrives from the Sun

 C longer wavelength than the radiation that arrives from the Sun

 D shorter wavelength than the radiation that arrives from the Sun [1]

Total Marks _____ / 15

Nuclei of Atoms

1 How many neutrons are there in a nucleus with this symbol $^{15}_{7}N$?

 A 22 B 15 C 8 D 7 [1]

2 What happens to the charge of a nucleus that emits an alpha particle?

 A it decreases by two C it stays the same

 B it decreases to zero D it increases by two [1]

3 Which of these cannot normally change an atom into an ion?

 A absorption of energy from electromagnetic radiation

 B high-energy collisions

 C gravity on Earth [1]

4 Which of these represents a beta particle?

A ^0_1e B $^0_{-1}e$ C ^1_0e D $^{-1}_0e$ [1]

5 What happens when an atom absorbs light?

A electrons can move further from the nucleus

B electrons can move closer to the nucleus

C electrons lose energy

D electrons move more quickly   [1]

6 Complete the sentence.

Alpha particles, beta particles and gamma rays are all kinds of:

A electromagnetic radiation.   B light radiation.   C ionising radiation.   [1]

7 Sketch an atom and show how:

a) it can gain energy without becoming an ion   [2]

b) it can gain energy and become an ion.   [1]

> Total Marks _____ / 9

Decay, Fission and Fusion

1 Which graph shows the longest half-life? **N** is the number of nuclei that have not yet decayed and **t** is time.

A 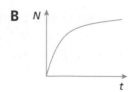   B   C 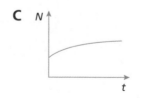   D 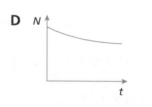   [1]

2 **HT** A sample of radioactive material contains 8×10^{24} atoms that have not decayed.

How many undecayed atoms will there be after four half-lives?

A 2×10^{24} B 1×10^{24} C 5×10^{23} D 2.5×10^{23} [1]

3 What is contamination?

   A exposing a material to ionising radiation

   B adding radioactive substances to a material

   C increasing the radioactivity of a material

   D absorbing energy from a material   [1]

4 For which of these purposes are radioactive materials **not** used in hospitals?

   A to kill bacteria

   B to kill cancer cells

   C to detect illness

   D to measure temperature   [1]

5 Complete the sentence.

   Fission and fusion both provide energy, because:

   A there is a chemical reaction with oxygen.

   B particles lose kinetic energy.

   C some of the protons and neutrons cease to exist.

   D a small part of the mass ceases to exist.   [1]

6 Different radioactive substances have different half-lives.

   a) What is a half-life?   [3]

   b) Some radioactive materials can be injected into human bodies so that illnesses can be
       discovered from outside the body.

       i)   Why would a material with a half-life of a few seconds be unsuitable for this?   [2]

       ii) Why would a material with a half-life of many years be unsuitable for this?   [2]

   Total Marks _____ / 12

Systems and Transfers

You must be able to:

- Understand that the total energy of a system stays the same unless energy enters or leaves it
- Recall that energy can be stored by systems and can transfer from one system to another
- Calculate the energy stored as thermal energy, as kinetic energy, as elastic potential energy or as gravitational potential energy.

Conservation of Energy

- In a car engine, fuel burns and so the temperature of the gas inside a cylinder rises.
- Pressure also rises and the gas can push a piston.
- If there is no other energy entering or leaving the engine, then the total energy available from the fuel is equal to the energy transferred to the piston.
- In reality, some energy is lost to the surroundings as heat.
- Even so, the energy available from burning fuel can never be destroyed – it just dissipates (spreads out).
- This is an example of **conservation** of energy.

Sources and Transfers of Energy

- Energy is released from a fuel when it is burned (reacting with oxygen in the air). Effectively, the fuel stores energy.
- There are other kinds of **energy store**.
- Water high up in a dam stores energy as **gravitational potential energy**.
- Flowing water is a store of energy until the energy passes from the water, e.g. to a turbine in a hydroelectric system:
  - The flowing water stores energy as **kinetic energy**.
  - The transfer of energy to a turbine is a **mechanical process**. Work is done.
- A stretched spring also stores energy, as does a bow.
- A bow can transfer energy to an arrow, so the arrow gains kinetic energy.
- The stored energy of a stressed object is called **elastic potential energy**.
- Energy flows from a hotter object to cooler ones around it. The hotter object acts as an energy store. The energy transfer processes, such as emission of radiation, are **thermal processes**.
- A battery or electric cell acts as a store of energy.
- Components in a circuit can transfer energy to their surroundings by heating (thermal processes) or by doing work (mechanical processes.)

Energy for Overcoming Resistive Force

- Energy is required to provide force over a distance to produce acceleration of a car.
- Energy is also required to overcome resistive forces – friction and air resistance.

Key Point

The energy of any system stays the same whatever happens inside the system, provided no energy enters or leaves. We say that it is conserved.

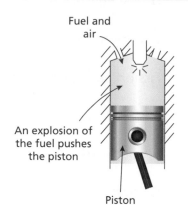

Fuel and air

An explosion of the fuel pushes the piston

Piston

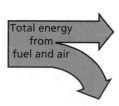

Total energy from fuel and air

Energy that does useful work on the piston

Energy that causes unwanted heating

Key Point

Resistive forces slow down a car and cause transfer of energy to the surroundings. The car will keep slowing until it stops, unless the energy is replaced.

Energy from fuel and air

For a car moving at steady speed on a flat road. Energy from fuel is just used to overcome resistive force. That causes heating.

Energy is dissipated—it's spread thinly into the surroundings.

Energy Calculation Summary

- The energy stored by a spring is equal to the work done in stretching it:

LEARN

> energy stored = work done (J) = force (N) × distance (m)

- Energy stored by a body raised above the ground is gravitational potential energy:

LEARN

> In a gravity field: potential energy (J) =
> mass (kg) × height (m) × gravitational field strength, g (N/kg)

- The gravitational field strength is about 10N/kg.
- Energy stored by a moving body is kinetic energy:

LEARN

> kinetic energy (J) = 0.5 × mass (kg) × (speed (m/s))^2

In this case, the force is the average stretching force and the distance is the extension of the spring.

- If one object is hotter than another, the hotter object acts as an energy store.
- Energy can flow from a hotter to a cooler object:

> energy available (to pass from hotter to cooler object) =
> mass × specific heat capacity × temperature fall

Use the mass, specific heat capacity and temperature fall of the hotter object.

- Energy transferred by an electrical component:

LEARN

> energy transferred (J) =
> charge (C) × potential difference (V)

This equation applies to energy transfer devices, such as a heater or motor. Remember, charge (C) = current (A) × time (s)

Quick Test

1. Energy cannot be destroyed, so describe what happens to the energy of a moving car when it stops.
2. Name **three** different kinds of energy store.
3. Calculate how much energy is effectively stored by:
   a) a kettle containing 0.5kg of water if the water is 70°C hotter than its surroundings
   b) a spring that is stretched by 0.05m by a final force of 15N
   c) 1000kg of water that is 50m above a hydroelectric power station
   d) a 0.03kg bullet moving at 400m/s.
   The specific heat capacity of water = 4200J/kg°C.

Key Words

conservation
energy store
gravitational potential energy
kinetic energy
mechanical process
elastic potential energy
thermal process

Energy, Power and Efficiency

You must be able to:

- Calculate the power of a device from data on energy and time
- Calculate the power of electrical energy transfer from data on current and voltage
- Calculate the efficiency of energy transfer processes.

Power

- **Power** is the rate of transferring energy:

> **LEARN**
>
> $$\text{power (W)} = \frac{\text{energy transferred (J)}}{\text{time (s)}}$$

Electrical Energy and Power

- Resistors are used for heating, e.g. in room heaters, cookers and kettles.
- Motors are used for doing work, e.g. in washing machines, vacuum cleaners, hair driers and power drills.
- The power of an electrical device is the rate at which it transfers energy. This is related to potential difference and current:

> **LEARN**
>
> **power (W) = potential difference (V) × current (A)**

- The unit of power is the watt (W).
- As a watt is quite small, the kilowatt (kW) is often used to measure the power of an electrical component or device.
- Rearranging the power equation gives:

> **LEARN**
>
> **energy transferred (J) = power (W) × time (s)**

- The standard international unit of energy is the joule (J).
- As a joule is quite small, the **kilowatt-hour (kWh)** is often used as the unit for energy transferred by electrical appliances.
- 1 kilowatt-hour is the energy that a 1 kilowatt appliance transfers in 1 hour.

Key Point

For calculations with answers in joules (J) for energy, the SI system of units, including amp, volt, watt and second, are used. For calculations with answers in kilowatt-hours (kWh) for energy, the kilowatt (kW) is used for power and the hour for time.

Efficiency

> total energy supplied =
>   useful output energy transfer + wasted or dissipated energy

- A ratio can be used to compare the useful energy output to the total energy supplied.

- Multiply the ratio by 100, to create a percentage figure, which represents the **efficiency**.

> **LEARN**
>
> $$\text{efficiency} = \frac{\text{useful output energy transfer (J)}}{\text{input energy transfer (J)}} \times 100\%$$

- A similar calculation involving power gives the same answer:

$$\text{efficiency} = \frac{\text{useful power output (W)}}{\text{total power input (W)}} \times 100\%$$

Increasing Efficiency, Reducing Dissipation

- We normally want efficiency to be as high as possible. That means that the wasted or dissipated energy must be small.
- Lubrication with oil reduces heating and dissipation in mechanical energy transfers.
- Old **filament lamps** are very inefficient. They produce a lot of unwanted heat.
- Compact fluorescent and **LED** lights produce less heat energy and are more efficient.
- We like our houses to be warm, but thermal energy transfers out from them, heating the world outside. The world outside gets only a very little bit warmer, because it is big. However, the energy lost from inside our homes is important.
- We **insulate** homes as much as possible to reduce energy loss, using materials such as foam boards. These have low **thermal conductivity**.

> **Key Point**
>
> All processes 'waste' some energy. The useful energy output is less than the energy supplied. The 'wasted' energy is spread thinly in the surroundings, often causing its temperature to rise by a small amount. The wasted energy is dissipated.

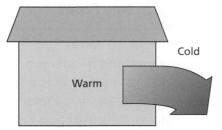

Poor insulation – high rate of energy transfer to the surroundings

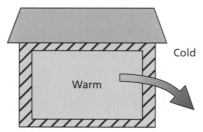

Good insulation – low rate of energy transfer to the surroundings

> **Quick Test**
>
> 1. An electrical room heater has a current of 5A and a voltage of 230 V.
>   a) Calculate its power in kilowatts (kW).
>   b) Calculate how much energy the room heater supplies to the room in i) 1 hour and ii) 6 hours. Give your answers in kWh.
>   c) Repeat question b), but give your answers in joules (J).
> 2. Calculate the efficiency of a motor that provides a useful energy output of 1kJ when supplied with 1.25kJ of energy.

> **Key Words**
>
> power
> kilowatt-hour (kWh)
> efficiency
> filament lamp
> LED
> insulate
> thermal conductivity

Physics on the Road

You must be able to:

- Estimate the sizes of some everyday speeds and accelerations
- Describe how to measure human reaction time
- Understand that when a driver makes an emergency stop, the total distance needed to stop is the sum of the thinking distance and the braking distance
- Describe the danger of large deceleration
- **HT** Estimate forces involved in car accidents.

Example Speeds

- If you walk quickly you can have a speed of about 1.5 metres per second (m/s). That's about 3.5 miles per hour (mph).
- A steady running speed for a fairly fit person is between 2.0 and 2.5m/s.
- An Olympic sprinter can run at about 10m/s.
- Acceleration at the start of a race is very important. A sprinter who goes from 0 to 1m/s in one second has an acceleration of 10m/s². If it takes two seconds, then the acceleration is only 5m/s².
- A fast but steady cycling speed is similar, although top cyclists can maintain an average of 14m/s for an hour.
- In a severe hurricane the wind speed can be 35m/s or more, but even a wind speed of 10m/s feels pretty strong.
- A commercial jet travels at about 140m/s, which is 500 kilometres per hour (km/h).

Human Reaction Times

- You can measure your **reaction time** by working with another person:
  ① They hold a ruler with its zero mark level with your open fingers.
  ② They let go at a random time and you close your fingers as quickly as you can.
  ③ The distance the ruler falls depends on your reaction time.

$$\text{reaction time} = \sqrt{\frac{(2 \times \text{distance ruler falls})}{g}}$$

- Air resistance doesn't have much effect because the ruler does not reach high speed.
- You can improve the accuracy of your result by repeating the measurement several times and working out a mean (average) value.

> **Key Point**
>
> When we sense something happening, we do not react at that exact instant. There is a short delay – our reaction time.

g is the acceleration of the ruler, which is the acceleration due to gravity and is equal to 10m/s².

Stopping Distances of Cars

- When a driver has to stop a car, first he or she must react.
- The distance the car travels during the reaction time is sometimes called **thinking distance**.
- Only after the reaction time does the driver actually apply the brakes. Then the car slows down.
- The distance travelled during braking is called **braking distance**.

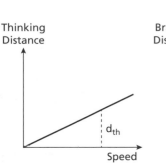
Thinking Distance vs Speed, d_{th}

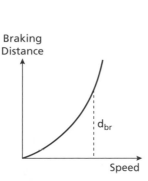
Braking Distance vs Speed, d_{br}

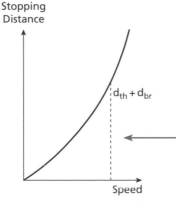
Total Stopping Distance vs Speed, $d_{th} + d_{br}$

The thinking distance, braking distance and total stopping distance are all bigger at higher speeds.

- The total (or overall) **stopping distance** is the thinking distance plus the braking distance.

Acceleration in a Car

- A car with high **acceleration** can reach more than 30m/s after just 10 seconds.
- The speed increases by an average of 3m/s every second. That's an acceleration of 3m/s^2.
- The acceleration needs a force.

 Key Point

When a car accelerates, you accelerate too. The car seat exerts a force on you. Remember: force = mass × acceleration

Deceleration During Accidents

- In a car accident, rapid **deceleration** takes place.
- Deceleration requires force, just as acceleration does, but the force is now in the opposite direction to the motion.
- The decelerating force can hurt and kill.
- Seatbelts and airbags decrease the decelerating force on passengers in an accident.
- A seatbelt is designed to stretch, while ordinary surfaces such as windscreens and steering wheels do not stretch in the same way.
- When a seatbelt stretches, it increases the time during which the deceleration acts, so decreases the deceleration and, therefore, the force.
- Airbags and crumple zones have a similar effect.

Key Point

Safety features such as seatbelts and airbags are designed to reduce the force that decelerates you in a car accident.

HT The force acting on your body during a car accident can be equivalent to 100 times your weight if you don't wear a seatbelt, e.g. if you weigh 500N, then the force is 50 000N.
HT That's the same force as a mass of 5 tonnes resting on your body.

 Quick Test

1. Calculate which is faster: a bullet that travels 100m in 0.4s or a plane that travels 1km in 3.3s.
2. Name the **two** distances that add up to make the total stopping distance of a car.
3. HT Write an expression for the force needed to produce a deceleration of 30m/s^2.

 Key Words

reaction time
thinking distance
braking distance
stopping distance
acceleration
deceleration

Energy for the World

You must be able to:

- Describe the main energy resources that are available
- Sort energy resources into renewable and non-renewable
- Explain why renewable energy resources are better for the future
- Recall that use of renewable resources has increased in the past decade.

Non-Renewable Energy Resources

- Electricity provides a convenient way of supplying energy to our homes, workplaces and leisure places.
- Electricity can be generated by burning **fossil fuels** – oil, coal and gas. Most of the world's electricity is generated in this way.
- However, once we take these fuels from the ground and use them, we can never replace them. They are **non-renewable**.
- **Nuclear fuel** also comes from the ground, from rocks, and is non-renewable.
- Nuclear fuel has the extra problem that it makes radioactive waste, which is very difficult to dispose of safely.

Renewable Energy Resources

- Wood is a **bio-fuel**. It will not run out, provided that we plant new trees to replace the ones we use – it is **renewable**.
- Other bio-fuels are produced from plant crops, such as oil seed rape and oil palm.
- Plants can store energy from sunlight by **photosynthesis**.
- We can use the energy that they store, but so far humans have not been able to create artificial photosynthesis.
- **Wind power** is also renewable.
- Winds in the atmosphere are caused by heating by the Sun, and by more heating in some places than others. As long as there is air and sunshine, there will be wind.
- **Hydroelectric power** stations generate electricity from moving water:
  - The water starts at a high point.
  - It travels down pipes to a lower point where it can turn turbines.
  - The water gets to the higher place by rain and, as long as there is water and sunshine, there will always be rain.
  - This energy source is renewable.
- Tides also produce natural movement of water, which can turn turbines.
- Energy can be taken directly from sunlight using **solar panels** that heat water or **solar cells** that generate d.c. electricity.
- Most countries in the world are trying to use more renewable energy and less fossil fuel.

Key Point

Fossil fuels are the remains of organisms from the distant past. The fuels were created by energy storage by the living things, which took millions of years. Humans have used a large proportion of the world's fossil fuels in a much shorter time.

Release of Carbon Dioxide

- The concentration of carbon dioxide in the atmosphere has increased over the last 200 years.
- At the same time, humans have burned more and more fossil fuels.
- The average temperature of the Earth has increased.
- The Earth absorbs energy from the Sun and emits it back into space. There is an energy balance when absorption and emission rates are the same.
- More carbon dioxide in the air makes emission of energy back into space more difficult, so it affects the Earth's energy balance.
- It is difficult to predict what will happen if we continue to add carbon dioxide to the atmosphere. It may produce a continuing **global climate change**.

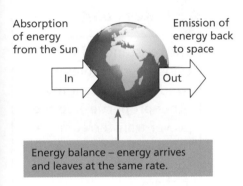

Absorption of energy from the Sun

Emission of energy back to space

In | Out

Energy balance – energy arrives and leaves at the same rate.

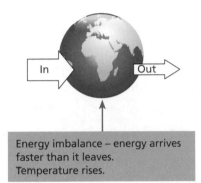

In | Out

Energy imbalance – energy arrives faster than it leaves. Temperature rises.

- Scientists are very worried about climate change.
- Politicians from all over the world have agreed to limit emissions of carbon dioxide from burning fossil fuels.
- There have been some changes, with increased use of renewable energy resources, but politicians sometimes find it hard to agree.
- Nobody is certain that the limits will be enough to prevent possible future climate change.

Quick Test

1. Group the following into **renewable** and **non-renewable energy** resources:
   A   wind
   B   tide
   C   nuclear fuel (uranium)
   D   coal
   E   bio-fuel oil
   F   gas (methane)
   G   hydroelectricity.
2. Explain why rapid release of carbon dioxide is a major problem for the future.

Key Words

fossil fuel
non-renewable
nuclear fuel
bio-fuel
renewable
photosynthesis
wind power
hydroelectric power
solar panel
solar cell
global climate change

Energy at Home

You must be able to:

- Explain that the transmission of energy from power stations uses transformers to reduce heating of the cables that wastes energy
- Explain the roles of live, neutral and earth wires in wiring in homes
- Recall that UK homes use electricity with a.c. frequency of 50Hz and a voltage of about 230V.

Transmission of Energy from Power Stations to Users

- Power stations can be a long way from the places where people live, work and play.
- The energy must be transmitted to where it is needed using cables. The network of cables is called the national grid.
- If there is a large current in the cables, a large amount of energy will transfer from them by heat, which isn't useful.
- The rate of transmitting the energy, or the power, in a circuit is related to current, voltage and resistance:

> **power (W) = potential difference (V) × current (A)**
> **= (current (A))^2 × resistance (Ω)**

- Fortunately, transmission can happen at high power using high voltage but low current. Then there is less heating of the cables and less energy loss.
- At power stations, voltage from the generators is made bigger using **step-up transformers**.
- High voltage in our homes would be dangerous. Near our homes, voltage is made smaller using **step-down transformers**.
- Transformers only work with a.c. (alternating current), so mains electricity is a.c. The current is always changing direction.
- Batteries and solar cells provide d.c. (direct current). This current is always in the same direction.
- In our homes, the voltage is about 230 volts (V). It is still a.c., and one cycle of alternation lasts $\frac{1}{50}$ of a second. The frequency is 50 hertz (Hz).

Key Point

The resistance of the transmission cables is fixed (by their length and other properties), so the power transferred from them is dependent on the square of the current in them.

Key Point

Transformers work using the changing magnetic field due to changing current in their coils. The current changes continuously – it is alternating current (a.c.).

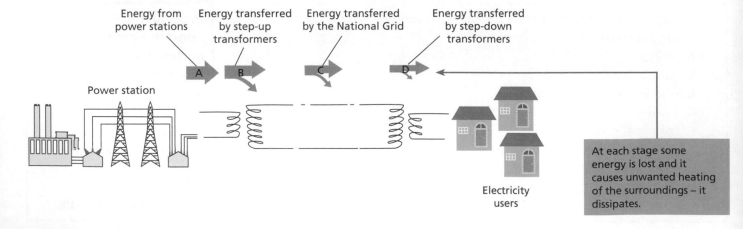

Energy from power stations | Energy transferred by step-up transformers | Energy transferred by the National Grid | Energy transferred by step-down transformers

Power station

A B C D

Electricity users

At each stage some energy is lost and it causes unwanted heating of the surroundings – it dissipates.

Electrical Wiring at Home

- There is a potential difference or voltage between a **live wire** and a **neutral wire**.
- When a resistor is connected between live and neutral wires it carries a current and it becomes hot – it's a heater.
- When a motor is connected between live and neutral wires the current and the resulting magnetic forces make it spin.
- If you touch a live wire, there is a potential difference between you and anything else that you are touching, such as the ground and there will be a dangerous current through you.
- If a live wire is badly connected inside the metal casing of an appliance then the casing becomes 'live'. Touching it can have the same effect as touching the live wire directly.
- The casing is earthed. It has an extra wire – the **earth wire**.
- There is a potential difference between the live wire and the earth wire. Normally they are not connected together, so no current flows.
- However, if the live wire touches the metal casing, a current can flow between it and the earth wire.
- As there is very little resistance between the live and earth wires, the current will be large.
- The large current can melt a deliberate weak point in the live wire connection – a **fuse**. This cuts off the live wire from the power supply, and makes the appliance safe.
- A fuse in the plug and the wall switch, next to the wall socket, can cut off the appliance from the live wire in the house circuit.
- However, the live wire in the house circuit still provides a potential difference and touching it is dangerous.

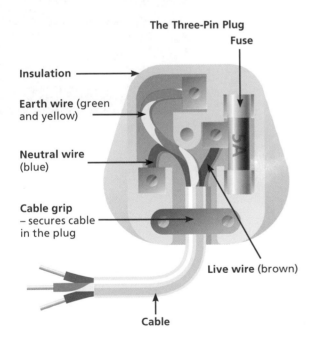

The Three-Pin Plug

Fuse

Insulation

Earth wire (green and yellow)

Neutral wire (blue)

Cable grip – secures cable in the plug

Live wire (brown)

Cable

Quick Test

1. Explain why electrical energy is transmitted using high voltage and low current.
2. Explain why electrical energy is transmitted using a.c. and not d.c.

Key Words

step-up transformer
step-down transformer
live wire
neutral wire
earth wire
fuse

Space

You must be able to:

- Explain why scientists believe that the universe is expanding
- Explain nuclear fusion in stars
- Describe how temperature affects the spectrum of radiation from stars
- Describe the range of objects that exist in our solar system
- Explain orbits of artificial satellites.

Evidence that the Universe is Expanding

- We can study the light from distant **galaxies**:
    - Their light is shifted towards the red end of the visible spectrum.
    - This means the light has a longer wavelength (and lower frequency) than expected.
    - The further away a galaxy is the greater this **red shift** is.
- Galaxies (except some nearer ones) seem to be moving away from us or **receding**.
- The further away they are, the faster they are receding.
- As a result, scientists believe that the **universe** is expanding.
- This leads to the idea that the universe began as a single point, a long time ago. That beginning is called the **Big Bang**.
- After the Big Bang, matter formed into atoms, and atoms formed into stars and galaxies.
- Ideas about the Big Bang predicted that the light of the very young universe should still be everywhere, but with low frequency and energy. It should be microwave radiation.
- In the 1960s, some scientists found exactly this kind of radiation – the cosmic microwave background radiation or CMBR.
- The discovery is evidence that the theory of the Big Bang is a sound one.

How Stars Form

- The Sun is a star. Stars like the Sun are made when clouds of dust, molecules and atoms collapse in together because every particle attracts every other by a weak force of gravity.
- The effect is large because there are so many particles. This is called **gravitational collapse**.
- Gravity crushes the particles together and they collapse into a small space, which makes the material extremely hot.
- The high temperature sets off nuclear fusion of smaller nuclei of atoms into bigger ones (see pages 64–65).
- The gravitational crush does not go on continuously because nuclear fusion, the high temperature, and the emission of light cause an outward pressure.
- There is a balance in the star, or **equilibrium**, between the gravitational collapse and the outward pressure.
- Stars turn small nuclei into bigger ones, by nuclear fusion; eventually they have too many big nuclei.
- They then lose their equilibrium and they die.
- Larger stars explode, while smaller stars expand and cool down.

> ### Key Point
>
> Red shift is evidence that the universe is expanding, and expansion of the universe supports the theory that it started from a single point.

Red Shift

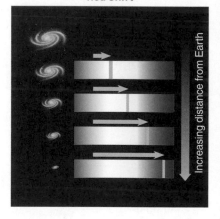

Increasing distance from Earth

> ### Key Point
>
> Stars form by gravitational collapse of huge clouds of gas.

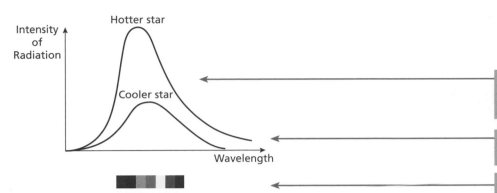

The visible Part of the
Electromagnetic Spectrum

A star with higher temperature can have higher intensity and bluer light than a cooler star of the same size.

Stars have different colours, depending on their temperatures.

Every body emits radiation. The higher its temperature the more energetic the radiation is. The radiation makes a range or spectrum of frequencies and wavelengths.

Planets, Moons and Other Objects

- Very many stars have planets in orbit around them.
- The Sun has eight, and also very many small objects.
- Some objects, including **asteroids**, **comets** and **minor planets**, have their own orbits around the Sun.
- Others – moons – are in orbit around planets, and stay relatively close to them as they travel around the Sun.
- Moons are natural **satellites** of planets.
- Our own solar system has eight planets: Mercury, Venus, Earth, Mars, Jupiter, Saturn, Jupiter, Uranus, Neptune. There are also minor planets, including Ceres and Pluto.

Artificial Satellites

- There are many artificial satellites in orbit around the Earth.
- We can use them for communication across the world or to observe the Earth's surface.
- Some satellites have **polar orbits**. They pass over both of the Earth's poles during their orbit. The Earth spins beneath them, so that in time they can scan across the whole planet. They are useful for observing the whole Earth.
- Some satellites have **geostationary orbits**. They orbit high above the equator at the same frequency as the Earth's spin, so they stay fixed over the same point above the ground.
- These are useful for communications, such as satellite TV. Receiving dishes can stay fixed, always pointing in the same direction towards the satellite.

HT The force on a satellite in orbit is gravity. It makes the satellite accelerate towards the Earth. However, the satellite doesn't fall down, because it has a large velocity parallel to the surface of the Earth.

HT The speed needed to keep the satellite in orbit gets smaller as the radius of the orbit gets bigger.

Quick Test

1. Explain why scientists believe that the universe is expanding.
2. What stops gravitational collapse of a star?
3. Name **one** example of **a)** a natural satellite of the Sun and **b)** a natural satellite of a planet.
4. Explain why geostationary satellites are useful for sending TV signals around the world.

Key Words

galaxy
red shift
receding
universe
Big Bang
gravitational collapse
equilibrium
asteroid
comet
minor planet
satellite
polar orbit
geostationary orbit

Review Questions

Sound, Sonar and Ultrasound

1 Complete the sentence.

The period of one vibration is:

  A the same as amplitude.

  B the same as frequency.

  C how long it lasts.

  D the length of a wave. [1]

2 Which of the following best describes a longitudinal wave?

  A direction of travel of the wave and line of vibration of the medium are the same

  B direction of travel of the wave and line of vibration of the medium are opposite

  C direction of travel of the wave and line of vibration of the medium are at right–angles

  D direction of travel of the wave and line of vibration of the medium are perpendicular [1]

3 HT Which of these statements is **false**?

  A Sound waves are longitudinal.

  B Water ripples are longitudinal.

  C Light waves are transverse.

  D Seismic waves (from earthquakes) can be transverse and longitudinal. [1]

4 HT In the human ear, what first detects arriving sound waves?

  A eardrum

  B small bones

  C cochlea

  D nerve to brain [1]

5 Which of the following best describes the movement of sound waves?

   A air vibrates and carries energy and information from the source

   B air vibrates and carries only information from the source

   C air travels from the source and carries energy and information

   D air travels from the source and carries only information   [1]

6 Which of these is **not** a wave detector?

   A an ear   **B** an eye   **C** a microphone   **D** a lamp   [1]

7 HT Which of these statements is **true**?

   A Sound waves are always produced by vibration of charged particles in electric circuits.

   B Sound waves and radio waves are always produced by mechanical vibration.

   C Radio waves are always produced by of charged particles vibration in electric circuits.

   D Sound waves and radio waves are always produced by vibration of charged particles in electric circuits.   [1]

Total Marks _____ / 7

Electromagnetic Radiation

1 Which of these statements is **true**?

   A Light waves always have the same speed.

   B Sound waves always have the same speed.

   C Sound waves can travel through space.

   D Light waves can travel through space.   [1]

2 Which of these is **not** part of the electromagnetic spectrum?

   A radio waves   **C** visible light waves

   B sound waves   **D** X-rays   [1]

Review Questions

3 Which of these are particularly hazardous?

   A infrared waves   **C** visible light waves

   B radio waves   **D** X-rays   [1]

4 Which of the following is the same for all electromagnetic waves?

   A amplitude in space   **C** speed in space

   B frequency in space   **D** wavelength in space   [1]

5 Why is it difficult to measure the speed of light?   [1]

6 **a)** Make a large sketch of the electromagnetic spectrum showing the main parts.   [7]

   b) Add notes to your sketch to show what different parts of the spectrum can be used for.   [7]

   c) Show which end of the spectrum has the longest wavelength and lowest frequency.   [1]

   d) Add notes to your sketch to show some hazards of some of the parts.   [2]

> **Total Marks** _____ / 22

Waves at Surfaces and Inside Materials

1 What causes refraction?

   A change of amplitude   **C** change of speed

   B change of frequency   **D** change of energy   [1]

2 Which of these diagrams shows the correct reflection and refraction of light at a block of glass?

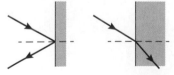
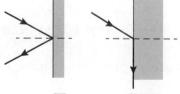

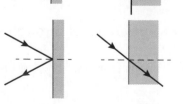

[1]

> **Total Marks** _____ / 2

Nuclei of Atoms

1 Which of these pairs are isotopes of the same element?

proton

neutron

[1]

2 Which of these are kinds of electromagnetic radiation?

A alpha particles   B beta particles   C gamma rays   D neutrons   [1]

3 What happens to the charge of a nucleus that emits a gamma ray?

A it decreases

B it decreases to zero

C it stays the same

D it increases   [1]

4 How does an atom become an ion?

A it loses or gains one or more electron

B it loses or gains one or more proton

C it loses or gains one or more neutron

D it loses or gains one or more gamma ray   [1]

5 When do atoms emit light?

A when electrons inside them lose energy

B when electrons inside them gain energy

C when alpha particles inside them lose energy

D when alpha particles inside them gain energy   [1]

Review Questions

6 What does 'random' mean?

    A in bursts   **C** very fast

    B without a pattern   **D** very slowly   [1]

7 Which type of radiation can travel furthest through a material?

    A alpha particles   **B** beta particles   **C** gamma rays   [1]

8 What is irradiation?

    A increasing the radioactivity of a material

    B absorbing energy from a material

    C adding radioactive substances to a material

    D exposing a material to ionising radiation   [1]

> **Total Marks** .... / 8

Decay, Fission and Fusion

1 Why can a substance with a long half-life be hazardous?

    A it stays radioactive for a long time

    B it emits radiation with especially high energy

    C it emits a high intensity of radiation

    D it loses its radioactivity quickly   [1]

2 Which of the following best describes nuclear fission?

    A the joining together of small nuclei

    B the splitting of large nuclei into separate protons and neutrons

    C the splitting of large nuclei into separate electrons, protons and neutrons

    D the splitting of large nuclei into smaller ones   [1]

3 What is the source of energy in the Sun?

    A reaction of hydrogen with oxygen   **C** nuclear fusion

    B nuclear fission   **D** radioactivity   [1]

4 Which of the following describes the nuclei in radioactive material?

    A stable   **B** unstable   **C** big   **D** small   [1]

5 When does a chain reaction happen?

    A when nuclear fission releases neutrons that can cause more fission

    B when nuclear fusion releases neutrons that can cause more fusion

    C when a radioactive emission releases neutrons that can cause more emissions

    D when ionisation releases neutrons that can cause more ionisation   [1]

6 Replace x and y with the correct numbers in the following equations showing radioactive decay.

    a) $^{x}_{6}\text{C} \rightarrow {}^{14}_{y}\text{N} + {}^{0}_{-1}\text{e}$ [2]

    b) $^{238}_{x}\text{U} \rightarrow {}^{y}_{90}\text{Th} + {}^{4}_{2}\alpha$ [2]

7 Draw a line from each symbol to the correct diagram.

    $^{2}_{1}\text{H}$

    $^{3}_{1}\text{H}$ proton

                                   ○ neutron

    $^{4}_{2}\text{He}$

    $^{3}_{2}\text{He}$ [3]

Total Marks .... / 12

Practice Questions

Systems and Transfers

1 Which of the following is **not** a store of energy?

   A a wind-up toy

   B water high in a reservoir

   C a moving bullet

   D burned ash on the ground   [1]

2 Water has a higher specific heat capacity than ethanol. From this information alone, which of the following is **true**?

   A it takes more energy to heat a kilogram of water by 20°C than a kilogram of ethanol

   B it takes less energy to heat a kilogram of water by 20°C than a kilogram of ethanol

   C it takes more energy to boil a kilogram of water than a kilogram of ethanol

   D it takes less energy to boil a kilogram of water than a kilogram of ethanol   [1]

3 Which of the following gives the SI units of work and energy in the correct order?

   A W and J   B W and W   C J and W   D J and J   [1]

4 Which of these transfers energy?

   A a battery in a circuit that is turned off

   B a resistor in a working circuit

   C a fuel in a car with the engine turned off

   D water resting in a high reservoir   [1]

5 a) How do you increase the gravitational potential energy of an object, such as your bag?   [1]

   b) How can an object lose gravitational potential energy?   [1]

   c) If an object loses gravitational potential energy, what happens to the energy?   [1]

6 Which of the following has the most energy?

   A a ball of mass 0.3kg moving at 20m/s

   B the same ball at a height of 200m

   C a spring stretched by 0.2m by a force of 300N   [1]

Total Marks _____ / 8

Energy, Power and Efficiency

1 An LED light has a power of 2W and a kettle has a power of 2kW.

Which of the following is **true**?

A The kettle transfers energy more slowly than the LED light.

B The kettle transfers energy more quickly than the LED light.

C The LED light stores energy more quickly than the kettle.

D The kettle must have a higher efficiency than the LED light.   [1]

2 Here is a diagram showing energy transfer by a system:

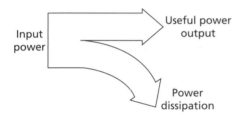

What can you say about the efficiency of the system?

A It is more than 50%.   C It is 100%.

B It is less than 50%.   D It is about 50%.   [1]

3 Which of these increases efficiency in a mechanical system?

A   conduction   B   dissipation   C   lubrication   D   convection   [1]

4 a) Calculate the efficiency of a motor that does 20J of useful work for each 50J
of energy that is supplied to it.   [2]

b) Explain what happens to the 'missing' energy.   [1]

5 a) These diagrams show energy transfers to the same scale. Which has the highest efficiency?

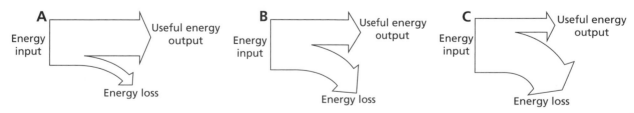

[1]

b) Explain your answer to part a).   [1]

Total Marks _____ / 8

Practice Questions

Physics on the Road

1 Which of these is closest to normal walking speed?

    A 0.2m/s   **C** 12m/s

    B 1.2m/s   **D** 24m/s   [1]

2 A train is moving at 10m/s and accelerates to 35m/s in 5s.

    Which of these is the train's acceleration?

    A $0m/s^2$ **C** $5m/s^2$

    B $1m/s^2$ **D** $10m/s^2$ [1]

3 In an emergency, what does the total stopping distance of a car **not** depend on?

    A the gradient or slope of the road

    B friction between the tyres and the road

    C the driver's thinking time

    D the speed of other cars   [1]

4 A car of mass 900kg is travelling at 20m/s.

    a) How much kinetic energy does it have?   [3]

    b) What happens to the energy if the car stops on a flat road?   [3]

    c) Why is the stopping distance longer when going downhill?   [1]

5 A cyclist has kinetic energy of 12000J.

    How much force is needed to stop the cyclist in a distance of 20m?   [3]

Total Marks _____ / 13

Energy for the World

1 Which of these is a renewable energy resource?

A coal   B gas   C oil   D wind   [1]

2 Which graph shows change in the use of wind energy resources in the UK over the last 20 years?

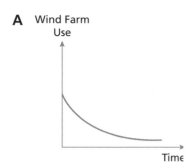

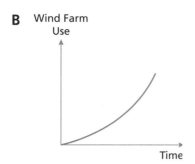

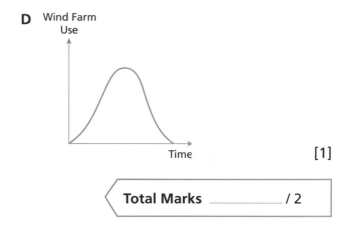

[1]

Total Marks .... / 2

Energy at Home

1 What is the voltage in UK homes?

A about 12V

B about 24V

C about 230V

D about 1kV   [1]

2 Complete the sentence.

A mains electric appliance and its on/off switch are connected between:

A the live and neutral wires.

B the live and earth wires.

C the earth and neutral wires.

D the positive and negative wires. [1]

3 Which graph shows alternating current (a.c.)?

A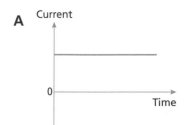

C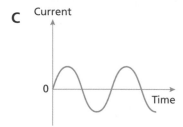

B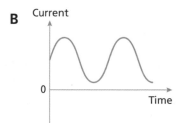

D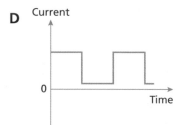

[1]

4 Why is it a good idea to send electrical energy over long distances using low current? [4]

Total Marks .... / 7

Space

1 What is red shift?

A a change in the speed of light due to the speed of distant galaxies

B a change in the wavelength of light due to the speed of distant galaxies

C a change in the brightness of light due to the speed of distant galaxies

D a change in the power of light due to the speed of distant galaxies. [1]

2 Complete the sentence.

Cosmic microwave background radiation (CMBR) provides evidence that supports ideas that:

A red shift happens.

B galaxies are receding.

C stars form when gravity makes clouds of dust and gas collapse.

D the universe began in a Big Bang.   [1]

3 Ceres is an object that orbits the Sun and does not orbit a planet such as Earth or Jupiter.

What is Ceres?

A a moon

B an artificial satellite of Earth

C a natural satellite of a planet

D a minor planet   [1]

4 What is the name given to the path of an artificial satellite that orbits the Earth at exactly the same rate as the Earth spins?

A lunar orbit

B geostationary orbit

C polar orbit

D unstable orbit   [1]

Total Marks _____ / 4

Review Questions

Systems and Transfers

1 Which of these statements agrees with the principle of conservation of energy?

   A Energy can be created and destroyed.

   B Energy can be created but never destroyed.

   C Energy cannot be created but it can be destroyed.

   D Energy cannot be created or destroyed. [1]

2 Which of the following does **not** supply energy to a system?

   A absorption of light   **C** using fuel to accelerate

   B emission of light   **D** heating [1]

3 What happens when a body accelerates?

   A it must experience a force, work must be done on it and it gains kinetic energy

   B it must experience a force, no work is needed and it gains kinetic energy

   C it must experience a force, work must be done on it and its kinetic energy stays the same

   D it must experience a force, work must be done on it and it loses kinetic energy [1]

4 Which of these is the kinetic energy of a car of mass 800kg travelling at 20m/s?

   A 400J   **B** 820J   **C** 1600J   **D** 160 000J [1]

5 How much energy is stored by 5×10^9 kg of water at a height of 500m?

   A 2.5×10^9 J   **B** 5×10^9 J   **C** 2.5×10^{13} J   **D** 5×10^{13} J [1]

> **Total Marks** _____ / 5

Energy, Power and Efficiency

1 What is dissipation of energy?

   A transfer of energy into surroundings so that it is no longer useful

   B transfer of energy into surroundings so that it can be stored

   C transfer of energy from surroundings so that it can be used [1]

2 A battery-powered motor uses 100J of energy to lift a load. The energy supplied to the load is 60J.

What happens to the other 40J of the supplied energy?

A it does work on the load

B it causes heating and dissipates

C it is stored by the motor

D it is returned to the battery   [1]

3 Which of these does **not** reduce the rate of unwanted energy transfer?

A lubrication

B thermal insulation

C dissipation

D streamlining   [1]

4 The table contains two examples of energy storage devices and systems and one example of an energy transfer device and system.

Give **two** more examples of each.

Energy Storage Devices and Systems	Energy Transfer Devices and Systems
battery arrow held in a bow	resistor

[4]

5 An electric current carries energy from a supply, such as a battery or the a.c. mains, to energy transfer devices in the circuit.

What are the main types of energy transfer in the following devices?

a) a heater   [1]

b) a motor   [1]

c) a hair drier   [1]

d) a lamp   [1]

6 Which of the following transfers the most energy?

A a 2.0kW kettle used for 5 minutes

B a 0.8kW washing machine used for 30 minutes

C a 400W television used for 2.5 hours   [1]

Total Marks _____ / 12

Review Questions

Physics on the Road

1 Which of the following measurements is closest to 100km/h?

   A 100mph   **B** 60mph   **C** 30mph   **D** 10mph   **[1]**

2 What is reaction time?

   A the time between an event happening and a person responding

   B the time between a person seeing an event and responding

   C the total time taken to stop a car after an event happens

   D the braking time of a car after an event happens   **[1]**

3 Which graph shows how thinking distance changes as speed increases?

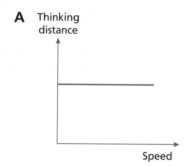

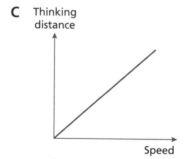

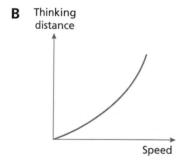

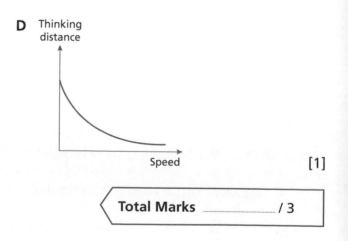

   [1]

> **Total Marks** _____ / 3

Energy for the World

1 **a)** Copy and complete this table adding at least **one** advantage and **one** disadvantage for each of the five different energy resources.

Energy Resource	Advantages	Disadvantages
coal		
oil		
wind		
solar		
nuclear		

[6]

b) Name **one** other energy resource and list its advantages and disadvantages. [3]

Total Marks _____ / 9

Energy at Home

1 What is the network of cables for transmitting energy over large distances called?

A national grid

B step-up transformer

C step-down transformer

D power station [1]

2 Complete the sentence.

50Hz is the:

A current of the mains supply in our homes.

B frequency of the mains supply in our homes.

C power of the mains supply in our homes.

D voltage of the mains supply in our homes. [1]

Review Questions

③ What immediately happens in an electrical appliance if the live wire becomes connected to the earth wire?

A the voltage becomes very large

B no current can flow at all

C a very large current can flow   [1]

④ Which of these is an electrical insulator?

A copper   C PVC

B iron   D steel   [1]

Total Marks _____ / 4

Space

① What does red shift of distant galaxies provide evidence for?

A the universe is expanding

B stars have different colours

C stars form when gravity makes clouds of dust and gas collapse

D light from stars speeds up as it travels   [1]

② What is electromagnetic radiation emitted by?

A no objects

B only very hot objects

C only radioactive materials

D all objects   [1]

③ What is the difference between:

a) a moon and a minor planet?   [2]

b) an asteroid and a comet?   [2]

4 Put these statements in order to provide an explanation of the Big Bang.

A Galaxies are moving away from us.

B Red shift happens because objects are moving away at high speed.

C The Big Bang theory predicted the existence of low energy radiation everywhere in the universe.

D Galaxies that are further away have more red shift.

E Cosmic microwave background radiation was discovered.

F The universe is expanding.

G More distant galaxies are moving away faster.

H Big Bang theory suggests that the universe exploded from a single point and is still expanding.

I The discovery supported Big Bang ideas.

J Light from stars has red shift. [6]

5 This graph shows the emitted intensity against wavelength for a particular star.

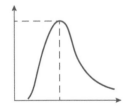

Which of these graphs shows the intensity against wavelength of a hotter star?

A
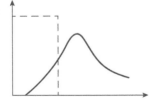

C
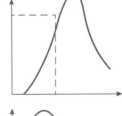

B
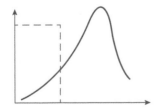

D
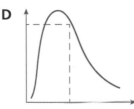

[1]

Total Marks .... / 13

Mixed Exam-Style Questions

1 Which one of these statements is **false**?

   A Visible light is electromagnetic radiation.

   B Visible light is ionising radiation.

   C Visible light carries energy.

   D Visible light travels as a transverse wave.   [1]

2 Dissipation of energy is reduced by which of the following?

   A having better insulation of houses

   B reducing the efficiency of an electric motor

   C using hot filament lamps instead of LED lamps

   D using step-up transformers to increase the voltage for long-distance
   transmission of electrical energy   [1]

3 Which one of these statements is **false**?

   A Electrons can orbit the nuclei in atoms.

   B Electrons can flow in wires to make electric current.

   C Electrons are the same as beta particles.

   D Electrons all have positive electric charge.   [1]

4 Which of the following has constant speed but changing velocity?

   A a car moving steadily along the road

   B the Earth in orbit around the Sun

   C a sprinter at the start of a race

   D a ball when you drop it to the floor   [1]

5 Some air is trapped inside a tube by a bead of liquid. The bead of liquid can move.

Jill places the tube in a beaker of water alongside a ruler.

She heats the water from 20°C to 90°C.

She measures the temperature and also the length of tube containing air.

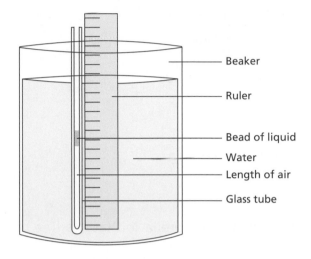

a) What happens to the volume of the air in the tube as the temperature rises? [1]

b) What happens to the mass of air in the tube? [1]

c) What happens to the density of the air in the tube as the temperature rises? [1]

d) What happens to the pressure of the air in the tube as the temperature rises? [1]

e) Jill plots a graph, with temperature on the *x*-axis (independent variable) and length of the air on the *y*-axis (dependent variable).

Sketch Jill's graph. [4]

f) A bicycle pump and a bicycle tyre also contain air.

When the pump is used to pump up the tyre, what happens to:

   i) the volume of the tyre? [1]

   ii) the number of molecules of air inside the tyre? [1]

   iii) the density of air inside the tyre? [1]

   iv) the pressure inside the tyre? [1]

g) HT A student pumps up a tyre and notices that the pump gets hot.

   Explain why this happens. [1]

6 This bus has a constant forwards velocity.

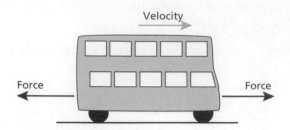

a) **i)** What is the net force acting on the bus? [1]

ii) What provides the forwards force? [1]

iii) What provides the backwards force? [1]

iv) What is its acceleration? [1]

b) A girl standing on the bus holds an umbrella so that it is free to swing.

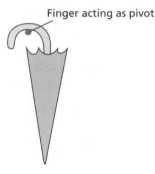

i) The girl notices that when the bus accelerates, the umbrella seems to swing backwards.

Explain why that happens. [1]

ii) What will happen to the umbrella when the bus decelerates to stop at a bus stop? You must explain your answer. [2]

c) **i)** A child runs in front of the bus and the driver brakes hard to make the bus decelerate. The girl falls forwards.

Explain why that happens. [1]

ii) What is the difference between the reaction time of the driver and the braking time of the bus? [2]

iii) How do we use reaction time and braking time to work out the stopping time of the bus? [1]

d) The moving bus has kinetic energy.

What happens to that energy when the bus brakes and stops? [3]

7 This diagram represents particles of gas in the space at the top of a bottle of fizzy drink. The arrows represent their velocities.

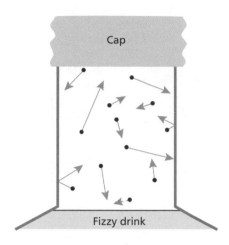

a) i) Why are the arrows different lengths? [1]

ii) Why do the particles move in straight lines? [1]

iii) What makes the pathways of the particles change? [1]

iv) What effect do the particles have on the walls of the bottle? [2]

b) If more gas particles rise out of the drink into the space, what will happen to:

i) the density of the gas? [1]

ii) the pressure the gas exerts (if temperature stays the same)? [1]

c) i) If the bottle of drink were stored in a refrigerator for an hour, what would happen to the pressure in the space if no more particles enter the space from the liquid drink? [1]

ii) Why do you hear a hissing sound when you open such a bottle of fizzy drink? [3]

d) i) What does 'compression' mean? [2]

ii) Name **one** use of compressed gas. [1]

iii) Liquids cannot be compressed. Instead they transmit pressure everywhere inside their container.

Give **one** use of this. [1]

8 This diagram represents an electric heater.
The supply voltage is 230V.

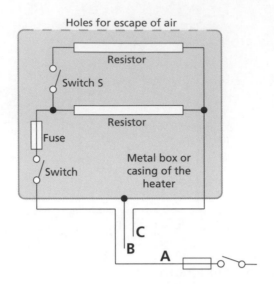

a) What do the resistors do? [2]

b) Are the resistors connected in series or in parallel? [1]

c) What is the purpose of Switch S? [2]

d) What are the names of the three wires: **A**, **B** and **C**? [3]

e) When all the switches are closed, a current of 4.6A passes through each resistor.

   i) What is the value of each resistor? [3]

   ii) What is their combined resistance? [2]

f) What is the maximum power of the heater? [3]

g) How much energy does the heater provide to a room in 3 hours? [3]

9 **a)** Sketch the magnetic field pattern around a simple bar magnet. [3]

b) HT How could you use each of **X**, **Y** and **Z** below to induce a voltage in the wire? [6]

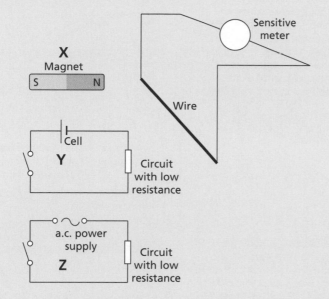

c) HT The frequency of the a.c. power supply in Z above is 1Hz.

 i) What effect will **Z** have on the sensitive meter when the circuit is switched on near the wire? [2]

 ii) What does Hz stand for? [1]

 iii) If the frequency is increased to 1kHz, how will the response of the meter change? [1]

d) HT **i)** Which system, **X**, **Y** or **Z**, is most similar to the principle of an alternator? Explain your answer. [3]

 ii) Which system is most similar to the principle of operation of a transformer? Explain your answer. [3]

e) Describe the roles of alternators and transformers in the supply of electricity to a computer. [5]

Mixed Exam-Style Questions

10 This diagram shows an ultrasound system used to examine an unborn baby.
The probe emits very brief pulses of ultrasound waves and detects reflections from surfaces, such as the baby's head.

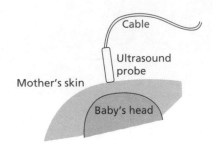

a) Explain whether or not ultrasound is:

  i) electromagnetic [2]

  ii) ionising [2]

  iii) transverse or longitudinal. [2]

b) The speed of ultrasound waves in the human body is about 1500m/s.

  If the time between emission of a pulse and detection of the reflection by the probe is 4×10^{-5}s, how far is the baby's head from the mother's skin? [4]

c) If the wavelength of the ultrasound waves is 5×10^{-4}m, what is their frequency? [3]

d) How can reflections be used to measure the speed of sound in air? [6]

e) Why are X-rays not normally used for examining unborn babies? [2]

f) X-rays can also produce images for examining inside human bodies, such as our chests.

  Explain how the principles of X-ray examination are different from the principles of ultrasound examination. [3]

g) How is sonar technology:

  i) similar to ultrasound technology? [2]

  ii) different from ultrasound technology? [1]

h) HT Seismic waves provide information about the inside of the Earth.

  How do the principles of this differ from the principles of ultrasound examination? [1]

11 The diagram shows light travelling through air and arriving at the surface of a material.

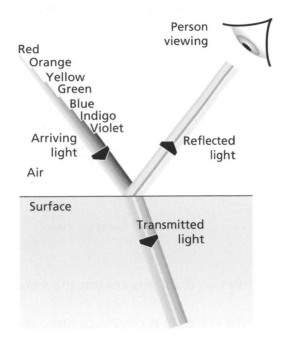

a) i) What colour does the person viewing see most strongly? Explain this. [2]

ii) What is the difference between red and violet light in terms of measurable quantities? [2]

b) i) What happens to the light that travels through the surface? [2]

ii) What happens to the energy of this light? [2]

c) i) Why does the transmitted light not continue in the same straight line as the arriving light? [2]

ii) Does light travel faster in air or in the material? You must explain your answer. [2]

d) Visible light is part of the electromagnetic spectrum.

What is the electromagnetic spectrum? [3]

e) How does your body respond to:

i) visible light? [1]

ii) infrared radiation? [1]

iii) ultraviolet radiation? [1]

iv) X-rays? [1]

v) radio waves? [1]

12 The diagram shows two houses. The temperature is the same inside them both. The arrows show rate of energy transfer out from the houses.

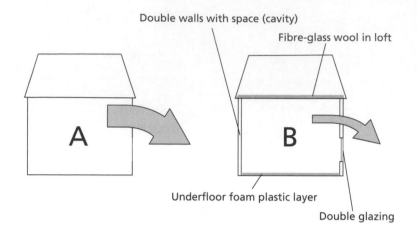

Double walls with space (cavity)

Fibre-glass wool in loft

Underfloor foam plastic layer

Double glazing

a) Explain why the arrows on the two diagrams are not the same. [2]

b) Why does the person who lives in House **A** pay much more money for heating? [1]

c) What happens to the energy that transfers out from the houses? [2]

d) What is another name for rate of transfer of energy? [1]

e) i) Name **three** energy sources that the people who live in the houses can use for heating. [3]

   ii) State whether the energy sources are based on renewable fuel, non-renewable fuel or a mixture of those. [3]

f) What are the advantages and disadvantages of using wind farms as sources of energy? [4]

g) What are the advantages and disadvantages of using oil as a source of energy? [4]

h) What changes in the use of different energy resources do you expect to happen in the next 10 years?
   Explain your answer. [2]

13 An artificial satellite is in geostationary orbit above the equator.

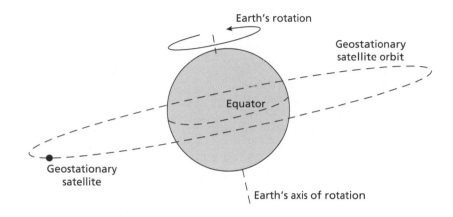

a) Draw an arrow on the diagram to show the direction of motion of the satellite. [1]

b) How long does the satellite take to complete one orbit of the Earth? [1]

c) The distance that the satellite travels in one orbit is about 360 000 km.

   i) What is its speed in km/h? [3]

   ii) What is that speed in m/s? [2]

   iii) Why are such speeds possible in space but very difficult near to the Earth's surface? [2]

d) Does the speed vary much during one orbit? Answer yes or no. [1]

e) Does the velocity vary much during one orbit?
   Explain your answer. [2]

f) i) What force keeps the satellite in orbit? [1]

   ii) Is the direction of the force always the same? Explain. [2]

g) This diagram shows the force acting on the satellite at one moment during its orbit.

   Copy the diagram and add arrows to show the velocity and acceleration for the satellite. [2]

h) The Earth has a natural satellite.

   What is it called? [1]

14 The diagram is a simple representation of the life cycle of a star.

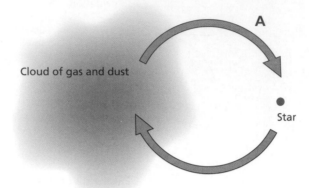

Cloud of gas and dust

A

Star

a) What causes change **A** to happen? [1]

b) The universe contains substances such as iron.
We can show one form of iron like this:

$$^{56}_{26}\text{Fe}$$

i) What does the 26 represent? [1]

ii) What does the 56 represent? [1]

c) This is a process that releases energy inside stars:

$$^{2}_{1}\text{H} + {}^{3}_{1}\text{H} \rightarrow {}^{4}_{2}\text{He} + {}^{1}_{0}\text{n}$$

n stands for neutron.

i) What is the name given to energy-releasing processes like this? [1]

ii) $^{2}_{1}\text{H}$ and $^{3}_{1}\text{H}$ are both hydrogen.

State the differences and the similarity between them. [3]

iii) Explain why older stars contain more iron than younger stars. [2]

d) This is another, similar, process:

$$^{X}_{1}\text{H} + {}^{6}_{3}\text{Li} \rightarrow 2\,{}^{4}_{Y}\text{He}$$

What are the values of **X** and **Y**? [2]

e) i) How can we know which elements exist inside stars? [2]

ii) How do observations of the same phenomenon tell us that the universe is expanding? [3]

15 This diagram shows pathways of three kinds of ionising radiation, travelling through air from three different radioactive sources.

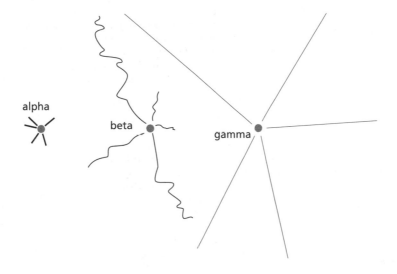

a) What does 'radioactive' mean? [3]

b) What does 'ionising' mean? [2]

c) Which kind of radiation travels furthest through air? [1]

d) i) Which kind of radiation runs out of energy soonest? [1]

ii) How can you tell this from the diagram? [1]

iii) Why does it run out of energy? [3]

e) Suggest why the tracks of the beta radiation are not straight lines. [3]

Total Marks _____ / 213

Answers

Pages 6–7 KS3 Review Questions

1. A   [1]
2. C   [1]
3. B   [1]
4. C   [1]
5. B   [1]
6. D   [1]
7. A   [1]
8. B   [1]
9. B   [1]
10. D   [1]
11. a) i) 1000kg   [1]
        ii) 2400kg   [1]
    b) mass = density × volume **[1]**;
         = 1000 × 0.01 **[1]**;
         = 10kg **[1]**
    c) 10kg   [1]
    d) The Moon has weaker gravity / lower gravitational field strength **[1]**; because it is smaller / less massive (than Earth) **[1]**
    e) i) reduces it   [1]
        ii) reduces it   [1]
        iii) no change   [1]
12. A2 **[1]**; B4 **[1]**; C5 **[1]**; D8 **[1]**; E7 **[1]**; F3 **[1]**; G1 **[1]**; H6 **[1]**

Pages 8–23 Revise Questions

Page 9 Quick Test

1. **Any three from:** Electrons are very small; have negative charge; in atoms they orbit the nucleus; they give an atom its negative charge to balance the positive charge of the nucleus; in metals some electrons are free to move between atoms but in electrical insulators there are no free electrons
2. Alpha particles were fired at atoms and some bounced back. That is only possible if atoms contain something very dense / bigger than electrons.
3. Positive
4. Electric force, between atoms
5. The electric forces between gases are almost zero, but the forces are strong in solids so it's very hard to push particles of a solid apart.

Page 11 Quick Test

1. Quantity that changes: internal energy (also, volume and density may change) Quantity that does not change: **(any one from)** mass; temperature; chemical composition; atomic structure

> Remember that in changes of state, atoms or molecules do not change. The forces between them and their internal energy change.

2. No. Changes in state involve changes of internal energy without the need for temperature change.
3. thermal energy for a change in state = mass × specific latent heat

= 267 000 × 1000
= 2.67×10^8J
(Accept 267 000 000J or 267 000kJ)
4. change in thermal energy
= mass × specific heat capacity × change in temperature
= 100 × 1006 × 10
= 1.01×10^6J to 3 significant figures
(Accept 1 006 000J or 1006kJ)

Page 13 Quick Test

1. Increasing the temperature of a gas increases its internal energy / increases the kinetic energy of each molecule. The particles move faster, hit (bombard) surfaces harder and more often.

> Remember that 'normal' means at right angles (90°).

2. Increasing the volume increases the space in between molecules / they are more spread out so each area of the surfaces holding the gas experiences a smaller rate of collisions.
3. Density of air decreases as height above the Earth's surface increases.
4. a) Objects sink when their weight is bigger than the upthrust on them.
    b) Upthrust is bigger on a fully submerged object than on a partly submerged one. An object floats on the surface when the upthrust is just the same size as its weight.

Page 15 Quick Test

1. kinetic energy = 0.5 × mass and speed^2
                         = $0.5 \times 0.5 \times 16^2$
                         = 64J

> Do calculations like these step-by-step. Always start by writing the equation. Then put in the numbers. Do the arithmetic and don't forget to write the final unit. If you try to do everything all at once you'll often get confused and make mistakes.

2. time $= \dfrac{distance}{speed}$

$= \dfrac{100}{40}$

= 2.5 hours
3. acceleration $= \dfrac{change\ in\ velocity}{time}$

$= \dfrac{(24-0)}{10}$

= 2.4m/s^2
4. 10m/s^2, which is the acceleration of free fall

Page 17 Quick Test

1. Gravity, or gravitational force (i.e. weight)
2. Electric or electrical force

3. Unbalanced (or net or resultant) force

> Remember that unbalanced force **always** causes acceleration of a body.

4. The skydiver falls a long distance and accelerates to high velocity. Resistive force increases as velocity increases. (Also, the surface area of the skydiver is large enough that the air resistance is substantial.)

Page 19 Quick Test

1. Zero and zero.

> The two balls have the same mass and the same speed. Because they are traveling in opposite directions, their momentums cancel each other out – the total is zero.

2. The ice skater experiences low resistive force (friction) so loses little energy, and needs to do little work to replace lost energy.
3. A person leaning on a wall exerts a force on it, but the wall doesn't move and there is no distance involved. Work = force × distance = force × 0 = 0.
4. Power is rate of transferring energy / power measures how quickly energy is transferred.

Page 21 Quick Test

1. They can change its shape / cause extension or compression.

> If the forces acting on a body are balanced then there can be no acceleration, but shape can change and this can be extension or compression.

2. a) elastic
    b) plastic
    c) elastic
    d) plastic
3. Physics concerns the whole universe, and weight for an equivalent mass is very different in different places. On the Earth's surface, the weight of a particular mass is much the same everywhere so the distinction is not relevant.

Page 23 Quick Test

1. Turning effect or moment = force × shortest distance. The distance between the force and the pivot is zero.
2. An object will be balanced when total clockwise moments are equal to total anticlockwise moments.
3. Levers can't multiply energy. The work done on the load can't be more than work done by the applied force. Work is force × distance, so if force on the load is increased by the lever then the distance moved by the load must be smaller.

> The load cannot gain more energy than is supplied to the lever. It's an example of conservation of energy.

4. pressure $= \dfrac{\text{force}}{\text{area}}$, so

   force = pressure × area. If pressure is the same but area is bigger, then force is bigger.

Pages 24–31 Practice Questions

Page 24 Matter, Models and Density
1. C [1]
2. D [1]
3. D [1]
4. B [1]
5. A [1]
6. density $= \dfrac{\text{mass}}{\text{volume}}$ [1];

   $= \dfrac{0.24}{0.0001}$ [1];

   $= 2400\,\text{kg/m}^3$ [1]
7. a) i) in the nucleus [1]
      ii) in the soft part of the cake [1]
   b) i) in the electrons [1]; in orbit (around nucleus) [1]
      ii) in the electrons [1]; embedded / inside cake [1]
   c) i) in the nucleus [1]
      ii) (spread throughout) the cake [1]

Page 25 Temperature and State
1. B [1]
2. A [1]
3. C [1]
4. Requiring energy: boiling [1]; evaporation [1]; melting [1]
   Releasing energy: condensing [1]; freezing [1]
5. They gain energy / they gain kinetic energy [1]; they move faster [1]
6. They can escape from each other / evaporate / boil [1]; they gain energy / they gain kinetic energy [1]; they move faster [1]
7. Steam has extra energy due to its state as well its temperature [1]; it transfers more energy to the skin [1]

> Remember that energy transfers to or from materials during changes of state **and** during changes of temperature.

8. a) mass (of the ice cube) [1]
   b) mass (of the water) [1]; specific heat capacity (of water) [1]

Page 26 Pressure
1. A [1]
2. D [1]

> Remember, g = 10N/kg.

3. a) Particles move faster / hit surfaces more often [1]; particles hit surfaces harder [1]
   b) Particles are further apart [1]; the rate of collisions with surfaces is reduced [1]
4. a) At greater depth, weight of liquid above is greater [1]
   b) Pressure on higher surfaces is smaller [1]; pressure and force act at 90° to surfaces [1]; force on higher surfaces is smaller, this results in an upwards resultant force [1]

Page 27 Journeys
1. D [1]
2. D [1]
3. A [1]
4. B [1]
5. D [1]
6. a) distance = speed × time [1]; = 24 [1]; kilometres [1]
   b) distance = speed × time = 40 [1]; miles [1]
   c) distance = speed × time = 4 [1]; × 3600 [1]; = 14400m [1]

> There are 60 × 60 = 3600 seconds in an hour.

   d) i) 24 000m [1]
      ii) 40 × 1600 [1]; = 64 000m [1]
7. a) A scalar has size, a vector has size and direction [1]
   b) **Any one from:** displacement [1]; force [1]; velocity [1]; acceleration [1]; momentum [1]
   c) **Any one from:** energy [1]; distance [1]; area [1]; speed [1]
8. a) speed $= \dfrac{\text{distance}}{\text{time}}$ [1];

   $= \dfrac{6000}{12}$ [1];

   = 500km/h [1]
   b) $500 \times \dfrac{1000}{3600}$ [1]; = 139 m/s [1]
   c) Direction changes [1]; including change due to curvature of the Earth [1]
9. a) The car experiences resistive forces [1]
   b) It projects material (gas), in the opposite direction to the acceleration / backwards [1]

Page 28 Forces
1. B [1]
2. C [1]
3. B [1]
4. Friction / resistive force [1]
5. A body can't accelerate without force / the acceleration of a body is proportional to the resultant force acting on it / force = mass × acceleration [1]
6. Any body that exerts a force on another itself experiences an equal force in the opposite direction [1]

Page 29 Force, Energy and Power
1. A [1]
2. D [1]

Page 30 Changes of Shape
1. B [1]
2. A [1]
3. C [1]

Page 31 Levers, Gears and Hydraulic Systems
1. A [1]
2. C [1]
3. a) moment = force × distance [1];
      = 18 × 1.5 [1];
      = 27Nm [1]
   b) force $= \dfrac{\text{moment}}{\text{distance}}$ [1];

      $= \dfrac{27}{0.3}$ (or similar working) [1];

      = 90N [1]
4. a) Balance [1]
   b) Rotation, anticlockwise [1]
   c) No (turning) effect [1]

Pages 32–41 Revise Questions

Page 33 Quick Test
1. Electric force can be attractive or repulsive.
2. a) Electrons are transferred to or from the surface by friction.
   b) Electrons can flow within the metal, and even our skin can conduct some electricity. So when we hold the spoon charge can flow to or from it and it doesn't stay charged.
3. Current is rate of flow of charge.
4. Current through resistance causes heating, so the surroundings are heated.

Page 35 Quick Test
1. A voltmeter measures the potential difference between two points.
2. a) An increase in voltage, or a decrease in resistance
   b) A decrease in voltage, or an increase in resistance
3. resistance $= \dfrac{\text{voltage}}{\text{current}}$. A metal wire's resistance increases when it is hot, so the ratio of voltage to current increases.
4. It decreases.

Page 37 Quick Test
1. a) total resistance = 2 + 4
      = 6Ω
   b) $\dfrac{1}{\text{total resistance}} = \dfrac{1}{2} + \dfrac{1}{4}$

      $= \dfrac{3}{4}$

      total resistance $= \dfrac{4}{3}$

      = 1.33Ω
2. They transfer energy by doing work (= force × distance) on objects outside the circuit, such as by lifting loads. (They may also become warm, and transfer some energy to the surroundings by heating.)

Answers

3. a) energy transfer =
       current × voltage × time
       = 1.5 × 12 × 60
       = 1080J

    b) power = current × voltage
       = 1.5 × 12
       = 18W
       OR
       power = $\dfrac{\text{energy}}{\text{time}}$
       = $\dfrac{1080}{60}$
       = 18W

Page 39 Quick Test

1. Sketch should show **looped** lines
    (magnetic field lines) that are closest
    together near the poles of the magnet.
    Arrows on the lines should point **away**
    from the north pole of the magnet and
    towards the south pole.

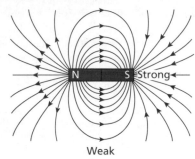
Weak

2. The shape of the magnetic field lines
    around a solenoid is similar to the shape
    around a permanent bar magnet but the
    field around the solenoid can be turned on
    and off by turning the current on and off.
3. Magnetic force due to interaction of
    the magnetic field around motor coil
    resulting from electric current and an
    external / separate magnetic field.

Page 41 Quick Test

1. A voltage is induced in the coil due
    to its movement through a magnetic
    field. The changing magnetic field
    experienced by the rotating coil
    induces an alternating current in the
    coil circuit.

    > Remember that a voltage is induced
    > whenever a conductor (such as a
    > metal wire) experiences change in
    > the surrounding magnetic field. The
    > change can be due to movement of
    > the conductor itself.

2. A voltage is induced in a secondary coil
    because it lies in a changing magnetic
    field that is caused by a changing
    current in a primary coil.

Pages 42–49 Review Questions

Page 42 Matter, Models and Density

1. D   [1]
2. C   [1]
3. A   [1]
4. B   [1]
5. C   [1]
6. Alpha particles (or small and fast positive
    particles) **[1]**; bounced back / deflected
    [1]; from gold atoms **[1]**; so it was
    concluded that atoms must contain a very
    dense region of positive charge **[1]**
7. a) density = $\dfrac{\text{mass}}{\text{volume}}$ **[1]**;
       = $\dfrac{1.0}{0.002}$ **[1]**;
       = 500kg/m³ **[1]**
    b) Yes, because its density is less than
       that of water (1000kg/m³)   **[1]**
8. a) **Any two from:** an atom has electrons
       / a nucleus does not **[1]**; an atom
       is neutral / a nucleus has positive
       charge **[1]**; an atom has low density
       / a nucleus has high density **[1]**; a
       nucleus has a very much smaller
       radius than an atom **[1]**
    b) An atom is neutral / an ion is
       charged or has charge **[1]**; an atom
       has equal numbers of protons and
       electrons, but an ion has different
       numbers **[1]**

    > Remember that in a neutral atom the
    > numbers of protons and electrons are
    > equal, but in an ion they are not.

    c) **Any two from:** an electron is much
       smaller / a proton is much bigger
       [1]; an electron has negative charge
       / a proton has positive charge **[1]**;
       electrons orbit the nucleus / protons
       are in the nucleus **[1]**
    d) Protons have positive charge **[1]**;
       neutrons are neutral **[1]**

Page 43 Temperature and State

1. C   [1]
2. D   [1]
3. A   [1]
4. D   [1]
5. C   [1]
6. C   [1]

Page 44 Pressure

1. A   [1]
2. Particles / molecules moving very fast
    [1]; bombard / hit surfaces **[1]**
3. Pressure decreases as height increases [1]
4. a) pressure =
       density of water × g × depth
       = 1000 × 10 × 15 **[1]**;
       = 150 000Pa **[1]**
    b) 150 000 + 100 000 **[1]**; = 250 000Pa **[1]**
    c) $\dfrac{250\,000}{100\,000}$ **[1]**; = 2.5 **[1]**

Page 45 Journeys

1. A   [1]
2. B   [1]
3. D   [1]
4. A   [1]
5. B   [1]
6. a) It has decreased   [1]
    b) It has decreased and changed
       direction   [1]
    c) Decelerated   [1]
    d) It is a braking / resistive force   [1]

7. a) acceleration = $\dfrac{\text{change in speed}}{\text{time}}$ **[1]**;
       = $\dfrac{30}{10}$ **[1]**;
       = 3m/s² **[1]**
    b) i) 0   [1]
       ii) kinetic energy =
          0.5 × mass × speed² **[1]**;
          = 0.5 × 1000 × 30² **[1]**;
          = 450 000J or 450kJ
                                                  [1]
    c) force = mass × acceleration **[1]**;
       = 1000 × 3 **[1]**;
       = 3000N **[1]**
    d) distance = $\dfrac{\left(30^2 - 0\right)}{\left(2 \times 3\right)}$ **[1]**;
       = 150m **[1]**
    e) work done = force × distance **[1]**;
       = (3000 × 150) **[1]**;
       = 450 000J or 450kJ **[1]**
    f) power = $\dfrac{\text{energy or work}}{\text{time}}$ **[1]**;
       = 45 000W or 45kW **[1]**

Page 47 Forces

1. B   [1]
2. A   [1]
3. D   [1]
4. a) Pushes / exerts a force   [1]
    b) i) little effect   [1]
       ii) it accelerates / moves   [1]
    c) **Diagram to show:** forces of the
       same size **[1]**; opposite directions **[1]**;
       acting on person and boat **[1]**

5. Gravity is too strong / weight is too big **[1]**
6. a) Large force to the right   [1]
    b) Smaller force than answer a to the
       right   [1]
    c) No net force   [1]

Page 48 Force, Energy and Power

1. C   [1]
2. a) work = force × distance **[1]**;
       = 180 × 2.5 **[1]**;
       = 450J **[1]**
    b) 450J   [1]
    c) Because of resistive forces / friction **[1]**

d) It gains gravitational potential energy **[1]**; of 300 × 2.5 **[1]** = 750 J **[1]**

Page 48 Changes of Shape
1. B **[1]**
2. a) weight = mass × g **[1]**;
    = 1.2 × 10 **[1]**;
    = 12N **[1]**
   b) i) 1.9(2)N on the Moon **[1]**
      ii) 30N on Jupiter **[1]**

Page 49 Levers, Gears and Hydraulic Systems
1. D **[1]**
2. A **[1]**
3. a) pressure = $\frac{force}{area}$ **[1]**;
    = $\frac{180}{0.2}$ **[1]**;
    = 900Pa **[1]**
   b) force = pressure × area **[1]**;
    = 900 × 0.8 **[1]**;
    = 720N **[1]**
   c) A small applied force can move a larger load / it multiplies force **[1]**
4. clockwise moments = anticlockwise moments **[1]**;
   300 × 1.5 = 200 × distance **[1]**;
   distance = 2.25m **[1]**

Pages 50–55 Practice Questions

Page 50 Electric charge
1. C **[1]**
2. C **[1]**
3. B **[1]**
4. C **[1]**
5. a) There are two kinds (negative and positive) **[1]**
   b) Two bodies with unlike charges **[1]**
   c) Two bodies with like charges **[1]**
6. a) Metals have electrons that are free to move, they are not all attached to individual atoms **[1]**
   b) Resistors resist the flow of electrons, so kinetic energy is transferred from the electrons **[1]**; resulting in an increase in temperature **[1]**

> Remember that resistors are energy transfer devices. They transfer energy out from a circuit by heating the surroundings. The energy then usually spreads into the surroundings, or dissipates.

   c) Some current can pass through each of the resistors **[1]**

Page 51 Circuits
1. D **[1]**
2. B **[1]**
3. C **[1]**
4. A **[1]**
5. A **[1]**
6. B **[1]**
7. D **[1]**
8. a) The cells are opposing each other **[1]**

   b) The diodes are opposing each other **[1]**
   c) The voltmeter is connected in series but should be in parallel **[1]**
   d) The positions of the switches mean that there is not a complete circuit **[1]**
9. a) To supply energy / create a potential difference or voltage **[1]**
   b) To measure current **[1]**
   c) To measure voltage / potential difference **[1]**
   d) To oppose current / to control current (or voltage) / or to provide heating **[1]**
   e) To allow current in only one direction **[1]**
   f) To change current (or voltage) **[1]**; depending on temperature **[1]**
   g) To change current (or voltage) **[1]**; depending on light brightness **[1]**
10. a) voltage = current × resistance **[1]**;
     = 1.5 × 6 **[1]**;
     = 9V **[1]**
    b) charge moved = current × time **[1]**;
     = 1.5 × 60 **[1]**;
     = 90C **[1]**
    c) energy transferred = current × voltage × time **[1]**;
     = 1.5 × 9 × 60 **[1]**;
     = 810J **[1]**
    d) rate of transfer of energy = power
     = $\frac{energy}{time}$ **[1]**;
     = $\frac{810}{60}$ **[1]**;
     = 13.5W **[1]**
    OR
     = current × voltage **[1]**;
     = 1.5 × 9 **[1]**;
     = 13.5W **[1]**

> Remember, units matter – never forget to include the unit with your answer.

Page 53 Resistors and Energy Transfers
1. B **[1]**

Page 54 Magnetic Fields and Motors
1. A **[1]**
2. D **[1]**
3. B **[1]**
4. C **[1]**
5. B **[1]**
6. The direction of force **[1]**; on a (small) north pole **[1]**
7. It affects magnetic needles / compasses **[1]**
8. It decreases **[1]**

Page 55 Electromagnetism
1. a.c. repeatedly changes between one direction and the opposite direction **[1]**;
   d.c. is always in the same direction **[1]**

> Sometimes it is not enough just to **know** something. You need to be able to apply your knowledge, such as knowledge of interactions between magnets and electromagnets, to be able to **explain** how something works.

2. The current in a coil **[1]**; varies **[1]**; the force between the coil and a magnet **[1]**; varies **[1]**; the current and force have a matching pattern **[1]**; the vibration of the speaker (cone) follows the same pattern **[1]**

Pages 56–65 Revise Questions

Page 57 – Quick Test
1. Vibrate
2. Frequency / wavelength – different pitch; amplitude – different loudness
3. Absorption is a transfer of energy from a wave to a medium (through which it travels). The wave loses energy / becomes weaker / even ceases to exist completely.

> Remember that a medium is a carrier, such as a carrier of information or energy. The plural word is media.

4. Transmission of waves through a medium and reflection by surfaces. They also rely on the fact that the speed of sound or ultrasound in a particular medium (such as water) is known.
5. There is always a region on the opposite side of the Earth to an earthquake where S-waves are not detected. S-waves can't travel through liquid.

Page 59 – Quick Test
1. Ripples are transverse waves, like light, but sound waves are longitudinal.
2. All electromagnetic waves have the same speed in a vacuum.
3. radio waves, microwaves, infrared, visible (red to violet), ultraviolet, X-rays, gamma rays
4. Frequency increases as wavelength decreases
5. Radiations with concentrated (or high) energy can pass this energy to electrons in atoms, so that the electrons become free from the atoms. Radio, microwave, infrared, visible and some UV radiations do not have sufficiently concentrated energy / Some UV, and X-rays and gamma rays do.

> Electromagnetic waves with higher frequency also have more concentrated energy.

Page 61 Quick Test
1. Transmission is the passage of waves through a medium. Absorption involves

Answers

transfer of energy to the medium by the waves.
2. They cease to exist. All their energy is transferred to the medium.
3. In reflection, waves hit a boundary with a new material but they return to the original medium. In refraction, waves pass through a boundary but experience a change in speed and, usually, a change in direction.
4. We observe most objects through the light they reflect (since they do not emit their own light).

Page 63 Quick Test
1. a) $^{12}_{6}C$, $^{13}_{6}C$, $^{14}_{6}C$
   b) Isotopes of the same element have the same number of protons, shown by the lower number, even if they have different total numbers of protons and neutrons, shown by the upper number.
2. Radiations carry a high concentration of energy, and when this energy is absorbed by atoms one or more of their orbital electrons can escape, leaving the atom as a positive ion.

Page 65 Quick Test
1. Fission is the splitting of large nuclei into smaller ones (and a few free neutrons). Fusion is the joining together of smaller nuclei to make bigger ones.
2. A short half-life means that the rate of emissions or decay by nuclei is high, so the material is very radioactive.

> A particular radioactive material has its own half-life. For a very unstable material that could be a tiny fraction of a second, and for one that's only a little unstable it can be very many thousands, or even millions, of years.

3. Materials with a long half-life can remain radioactive in the environment for long times.
4. A contaminated material contains some radioactive material.
5. $\frac{N}{8}$ **[1]**

Pages 66–71 **Review Pages**

Page 66 Electric charge
1. D **[1]**
2. D **[1]**
3. A **[1]**
4. B **[1]**
5. B **[1]**
6. B **[1]**
7. B **[1]**

Page 67 Circuits
1. A diode **[1]**
2. A **[1]**

3. a) A kilovolt is 1000 volts. **[1]**
   b) A battery has more than one cell. **[1]**
   c) In series circuits the current passes through one component after another, but in a parallel circuit it passes through one or the other / the current divides. **[1]**

> If resistors are connected in parallel then adding more of them **decreases** total resistance because the current has more routes to follow.

   d) An ammeter measures current; a voltmeter measures voltage or potential difference. **[1]**
   e) The ammeter is connected in series with the component; the voltmeter is connected across it, in parallel with it. **[1]**
4. a) Circuit drawn with: cell or battery and switch **[1]**; ammeter **[1]**; filament lamp **[1]**; the components all in a series **[1]**; voltmeter in parallel with the lamp **[1]**

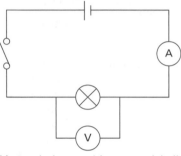

   b) Graph drawn with: current labelled on y-axis **[1]**; voltage labelled on x-axis **[1]**; line is straight at low current **[1]**; line becomes curved, towards the voltage axis **[1]**

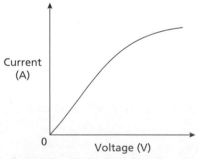

   c) Resistance is higher when the wire is hot **[1]**; due to increased difficulty of electron flow **[1]**

Page 68 Resistors and Energy Transfers
1. D **[1]**
2. a) It decreases **[1]**
   b) It increases **[1]**
3. a) Power **[1]**
   b) energy = power × time **[1]**;
      = 2 × 2.5 **[1]**;
      = 5kWh **[1]**

> Remember that the kilowatt-hour, kWh, is a unit of energy but the kilowatt, kW, is a unit of power.

   c) Second **[1]**; joule **[1]**
   d) The SI units are small **[1]**
   e) energy = power × time
      = 2000 × 2.5 × 3600 **[1]**;
      = 18 000 000J or 1.8×10^7J **[1]**

Page 69 Magnetic Fields and Motors
1. C **[1]**
2. C **[1]**
3. Bring a compass close to the coil **[1]**; the compass will point along the magnetic field lines of the coil **[1]**
4. More turns in the coil **[1]**; more current in the coil **[1]**; have an iron core inside the coil **[1]**
5. force = magnetic flux density × current × length
   = 0.12 × 2.5 × 0.15 **[1]**;
   = 0.045N **[1]**
6. The force on one side of the coil **[1]**; must be upwards to match its upwards movement **[1]**; and downwards to match its downwards movement **[1]**; the field is always in the same direction **[1]**; so the current must reverse in direction **[1]**; every half turn **[1]**

Page 70 Electromagnetism
1. D **[1]**
2. B **[1]**
3. D **[1]**
4. A **[1]**
5. A **[1]**
6. a) To provide a changing magnetic field **[1]**
   b) Voltage is induced **[1]**
   c) Step-down **[1]**
   d) 24V **[1]**
7. a) It varies in a pattern that matches the original sound **[1]**
   b) The varying current creates a varying force on the coil in a magnetic field **[1]**; which makes (the cone of) the loudspeaker vibrate **[1]**

Pages 72–77 **Practice Pages**

Page 72 Sound, Sonar and Ultrasound
1. B **[1]**
2. A **[1]**
3. C **[1]**
4. C **[1]**
5. D **[1]**
6. B **[1]**
7. B **[1]**
8. C **[1]**
9. A **[1]**
10. D **[1]**
11. A **[1]**
12. D **[1]**

Page 73 Electromagnetic Radiation
1. A **[1]**
2. B **[1]**
3. D **[1]**

4. speed = frequency × wavelength [1];
   = $(4 \times 10^{14}) \times (5 \times 10^{-7})$ [1];
   = 2×10^8 m/s [1] (Accept 200 000 000m/s)

> Using powers of ten for very large and very small numbers is easier than writing numbers in full and counting the zeros.

Page 74 Waves at Surfaces and Inside Materials

1. Frequency: stays the same [1]; Wavelength: changes [1]
2. a) Reflection [1]; refraction [1]
   b) Transmission [1]; absorption [1]; scattering [1]
3. Reflection with equal angles [1]; refraction with smaller angle (to normal line) in glass [1]; normal lines drawn [1]

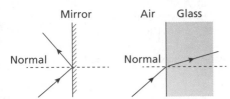

4. Reflection with equal angles resulting in convergence [1]; refraction with smaller angle in denser medium resulting in divergence [1]; (at least some) normal lines drawn [1]

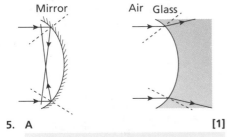

5. A [1]

> Remember that a ray is a line drawn to show the direction of travel of a wave.

6. C [1]

Page 75 Nuclei of Atoms

1. C [1]
2. A [1]
3. C [1]
4. B [1]
5. A [1]

> To move further away from a nucleus, an electron must gain energy. If it escapes completely the atom is ionised.

6. C [1]
7. a) Atom with electron orbits [1]; representation of movement of electron to higher orbit [1]
   b) Representation of removal of electron from atom [1]

Page 76 Decay, Fission and Fusion

1. D [1]
2. C [1]
3. B [1]
4. D [1]
5. D [1]
6. a) The time taken [1]; for half [1]; of the radioactive nuclei to decay [1]
   b) i) No time to examine the patient before radioactivity is too small [1]; patient exposed to unnecessary levels of radiation [1]
      ii) Would need to give large amount to patient [1]; material would remain in patient or the environment for a long time [1]

Pages 78–89 Revise Pages

Page 79 Quick Test

1. The energy is transferred to the environment, such as in moving air, and eventually spreads thinly causing heating of the environment (air, road). The energy dissipates / is dissipated.
2. **Any three from:** gravitational potential energy of a raised mass; kinetic energy of a moving mass; elastic potential energy of a stretched or compressed object; thermal energy of a hot object; electric potential energy of a battery
3. a) energy available to transfer to surroundings = mass × specific heat capacity × temperature difference
   = $0.5 \times 4200 \times 70$
   = 147 000J **OR**
   = 147kJ
   b) energy stored = (average) force × distance (extension)
   = $\left(\dfrac{15}{2}\right) \times 0.5$
   = 0.375J
   c) potential energy = mass × height × g
   = $1000 \times 50 \times 10$
   = 500 000J **OR**
   = 500kJ
   d) kinetic energy = $0.5 \times$ mass × speed^2
   = $0.5 \times 0.03 \times 400^2$
   = 2400J **OR**
   = 2.4kJ

Page 81 Quick Test

1. a) power = current × potential difference
   = 5×230
   = 1150W = 1.15kW
   b) i) energy = power × time
   = 1.15×1
   = 1.15kWh
   ii) energy = power × time
   = 1.15×6
   = 6.9kWh
   c) i) energy = power × time
   = 1150×3600
   = 4 140 000J **OR**
   = 4.14×10^6J

ii) $4 140 000 \times 6 = 24 840 000$J **OR**
   $2.48(4) \times 10^7$J

2. efficiency = $\dfrac{\text{useful output energy transfer}}{\text{input energy transfer}} \times 100\%$
   = $\dfrac{1}{1.25} \times 100\%$
   = 80%

Page 83 Quick Test

1. speed = $\dfrac{\text{distance}}{\text{time}}$
   For the bullet: speed = $\dfrac{100}{0.4}$
   = 250m/s
   For the plane: speed = $\dfrac{1000}{3.3}$
   = 303m/s
   The plane is faster.
2. Thinking distance and braking distance

> During thinking time speed is constant, but during braking time speed is decreasing.

3. If your mass is Xkg, then force needed
   = mass × acceleration
   = X × 30
   = 30X N

Page 85 Quick Test

1. Renewable: A, B, E and G
   Non-renewable: C, D and F
2. Carbon dioxide makes it harder for the atmosphere / Earth to emit energy back into space. This can cause global climate change.

Page 87 Quick Test

1. High current in cables causes heating. That means that the system loses a lot of energy. By transmitting at low current this energy loss is reduced. The power output from the power station is voltage × current, so if the current is to be low then the voltage needs to be high.
2. Transformers can transfer energy from one circuit to another. They allow energy to be transmitted at high voltage (stepped up) and then received by users at lower voltage (stepped down). But they don't work if the current in the transformers themselves is steady – it has to change. a.c. is continuously changing.

Page 89 Quick Test

1. Red shift of light from galaxies shows that they are receding from us. The red shift is bigger for more distant galaxies.

Answers

2. Outward pressure due to fusion / emission of light

> Remember, stars experience equilibrium between this outward pressure and the huge inward pressure caused by gravity.

3. **a)** A planet / any named planet
   b) A moon / any named moon
4. A geostationary satellite always appears in the same place because it rotates with the Earth. The TV transmitter and the receiver can always point to the same point in the sky.

Pages 90–95 Review Questions

Page 90 Sound, Sonar and Ultrasound
1. C [1]
2. A [1]
3. B [1]
4. A [1]
5. A [1]
6. D [1]
7. C [1]

Page 91 Electromagnetic Radiation
1. D [1]
2. B [1]
3. D [1]
4. C [1]

> Spectrum means 'range'. Electromagnetic waves have a range of wavelengths and range of frequencies, but they all have the same speed in space.

5. The speed of light is very high [1]
6. **a) The sketch should show:** radio [1]; microwaves [1]; infrared [1]; visible [1]; ultraviolet [1]; X-rays [1]; gamma rays [1] **(this order required, or its reverse)**

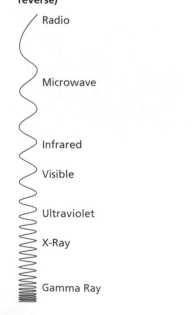

Radio

Microwave

Infrared

Visible

Ultraviolet

X-Ray

Gamma Ray

b) Radio – communications [1]; microwaves – communications / cooking [1]; infrared – heating [1]; visible – seeing [1]; ultraviolet – security marking [1]; X-rays – medical imaging [1]; gamma rays – killing bacteria / treating tumours / medical imaging [1]
c) The radio end of the spectrum [1]
d) Any two from: ultraviolet – skin damage / cancer [1]; X-rays – tissue damage / cancer [1]; gamma rays – tissue damage / cancer [1]
7. C [1]

Page 92 Waves at Surfaces and Inside Materials
1. C [1]
2. B [1]

Page 93 Nuclei of Atoms
1. A [1]
2. C [1]
3. C [1]
4. A [1]
5. A [1]

> Less penetrating radiations lose energy more quickly as they travel through a medium or substance. They pass the energy to the medium.

6. B [1]
7. C [1]
8. D [1]

Page 94 Decay, Fission and Fusion
1. A [1]
2. D [1]
3. C [1]
4. B [1]
5. A [1]
6. **a)** $x = 14$ [1]; $y = 7$ [1]
   b) $x = 92$ [1]; $y = 234$ [1]
7. Four correctly drawn lines [3] (2 marks for two correct lines; 1 mark for one)

$^2_1$H

$^3_1$H

$^4_2$He

$^3_2$He

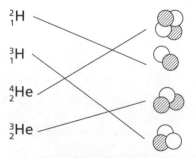

Pages 96–101 Practice Questions

Page 96 Systems and Transfers
1. D [1]
2. A [1]
3. D [1]
4. B [1]
5. **a)** Lift it [1]
   b) By falling [1]

c) It is transferred to kinetic energy and then the bag may do work / cause a temperature rise / produce a sound on hitting something [1]
6. B [1]

Page 97 Energy, Power and Efficiency
1. B [1]
2. D [1]
3. C [1]
4. **a)** $\text{efficiency} = \dfrac{\text{useful output energy transfer}}{\text{input energy transfer}} \times 100$

   $= \dfrac{20}{50} \times 100$ [1];

   $= 40\%$ [1]
   b) It causes heating / temperature rise / it dissipates [1]
5. **a)** A [1]
   b) The 'lost energy' is a smaller proportion [1]

Page 98 Physics on the Road
1. B [1]
2. C [1]
3. D [1]
4. **a)** $\text{kinetic energy} = 0.5 \times \text{mass} \times \text{speed}^2$ [1];

   $= 0.5 \times 900 \times 20^2$ [1];

   $= 180\,000\text{J or }180\text{kJ}$ [1]
   b) It transfers to the surroundings / dissipates [1]; (mostly) through the brakes [1]; (mostly) causing heating [1]
   c) The car has gravitational potential energy to dissipate as well as its kinetic energy. [1]
5. work = force × distance,

   $\text{force} = \dfrac{\text{work}}{\text{distance}}$ [1];

   $= \dfrac{12\,000}{20}$ [1]; $= 600\text{N}$ [1]

Page 99 Energy for the World
1. D [1]
2. B [1]

Page 99 Energy at Home
1. C [1]
2. A [1]
3. C [1]
4. Wires get hot and the bigger the current the hotter they get [1]; the heating transfers energy to the surroundings [1]; that energy is wasted [1]; so using low current reduces energy loss to the surroundings. [1]

Page 100 Space
1. B [1]
2. D [1]
3. D [1]
4. B [1]

Answers

Pages 102–107 Review Questions

Page 102 Systems and Transfers
1. D [1]
2. B [1]
3. A [1]
4. D [1]
5. C [1]

Page 102 Energy, Power and Efficiency
1. A [1]
2. B [1]
3. C [1]
4. Energy storage devices and systems – **any two from:** water in a reservoir [1]; fuel [1]; a hot kettle [1]; any moving object [1]; Energy transfer devices and systems – **any two from:** motor [1]; lamp [1]; engine [1]; any electrical appliance [1]

> A resistor with a steady current receives energy just as quickly as it passes energy to the surroundings by heating. It doesn't store energy.

5. a) heating [1]
   b) working [1]
   c) heating and working [1]
   d) emitting light [1]
6. C [1]

Page 104 Physics on the Road
1. B [1]
2. A [1]
3. C [1]

Page 105 Energy for the World
1. a) 1 mark for each advantage / disadvantage (maximum of 6 points; for full marks there must be a balance of advantages and disadvantages)

Energy resource	Advantages	Disadvantages
coal	• cheap • still a lot in the ground	• causes pollution • releases carbon dioxide
oil	• cheap • convenient, widely usable • still a lot available	• causes pollution • releases carbon dioxide
wind	• renewable • clean	• requires large wind farms
solar	• renewable • good for local supply	• only suitable for mass use if large solar farms are built • expensive
nuclear	• uses little fuel • no polluting emissions	• produces radioactive waste material • expensive

b) Any one resource, plus one advantage and one disadvantage, from: gas [1]; advantage – widely available [1]; disadvantage – burning releases carbon dioxide [1]; bio-fuel [1]; advantage – renewable [1]; disadvantage – large land use needed [1]; hydroelectric [1]; advantage – renewable [1]; disadvantage – needs high dammed reservoirs [1]; tides [1]; advantage – renewable / always available [1]; disadvantage – barrage needed across estuary [1]

Page 105 Energy at Home
1. A [1]
2. B [1]
3. C [1]
4. C [1]

Page 106 Space
1. A [1]
2. D [1]
3. a) Moons orbit planets [1]; minor planets orbit the Sun [1]
   b) Most asteroids stay in a belt (between Mars and Jupiter) and do not pass close to the Sun [1]; comets travel from very far away in the Solar System but can pass close to the Sun [1]
4. J, B, A, D, G, F, H, C, E, I [6] (4 marks for more than five in the correct order; 2 marks for more than three in the correct order)
5. D [1]

Pages 108–119 Mixed Exam-Style Questions

1. B [1]
2. A [1]
3. D [1]
4. B [1]
5. a) Increases [1]
   b) Stays the same [1]
   c) Decreases [1]
   d) Stays the same [1]
   e) x-axis labelled temperature [1]; y-axis labelled length [1]; straight line [1]; with intercept on y-axis [1]

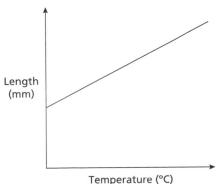

Length (mm) vs Temperature (°C)

   f) i) No change / small change / small increase [1]
      ii) Increases [1]
      iii) Increases [1]
      iv) Increases [1]
   g) work is done (on the air) [1]
6. a) i) Zero [1]
      ii) Driving force / engine [1]
      iii) Resistance (air, friction) [1]
      iv) Zero [1]
   b) i) Inertia / resistance to acceleration / need for a force for acceleration [1]
      ii) Swing forward [1]; inertia / resistance to deceleration / need for a force for deceleration [1]
   c) i) Inertia / resistance to deceleration / need for a force for deceleration [1]
      ii) Reaction time – time between event and driver acting [1]; braking time – time between driver acting and vehicle stopping [1]
      iii) Add them together [1]
   d) Heating [1]; in brakes (and / or road, air) [1]; dissipation / spread thinly in surroundings [1]
7. a) i) Different speeds [1]
      ii) No forces (to make motion change) [1]
      iii) Collisions [1]
      iv) Exert pressure [2] (Accept 'force' for 1 mark) [2]
   b) i) Increases [1]
      ii) Increases [1]
   c) i) Decreases [1]
      ii) Gas pressure [1]; higher than atmospheric pressure [1]; gas flows out [1]
   d) i) Reducing volume [1]; by applying pressure [1]
      ii) **Any one from:** in aerosol spray cans [1]; in breathing apparatus for diving [1] (Accept any other good use)
      iii) **Any one from:** hydraulic systems [1]; force multiplication / lifting large loads [1]
8. a) Oppose current [1]; and produce heating (electrical energy is transferred to heat) [1]
   b) In parallel [1]
   c) To switch the supply to second resistor on and off [1]; control heating / turn heater up [1]
   d) A = live [1]; B = earth [1]; C = neutral [1]
   e) i) resistance $= \dfrac{\text{potential difference}}{\text{current}}$ [1]
      $= \dfrac{230}{4.6}$ [1];
      $= 50\Omega$ [1]
      ii) $\dfrac{1}{R_t} = \dfrac{1}{R_1} + \dfrac{1}{R_2}$
      $= \dfrac{1}{50} + \dfrac{1}{50} = \dfrac{1}{25}$ [1];
      $R_t = \dfrac{25}{1} = 25\Omega$ [1]

Answers

f) power =
potential difference × current [1];
= 9.2 × 230 [1];
= 2116W [1]

g) energy transferred = power × time [1];
= 2.116 × 3 [1];
= 6.35kWh [1]

9. a) Correct sketch with north and south poles labelled [1]; arrows pointing away from north pole and towards south pole [1]; with looped field lines that get further apart as they move away from the magnet [1]

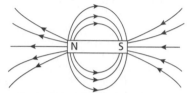

b) X: move it quickly [1]; near wire [1];
Y: turn on [1]; or off [1];
Z: turn on [1]; close to wire [1]

c) i) The meter (needle) will move backwards and forwards [1]; at 1Hz [1]

ii) Hertz (1Hz = 1 cycle per second) [1]

iii) It will not have time to respond / may vibrate / show no reading [1]

d) i) X [1]; because the wire is in changing magnetic field [1]; due to relative movement of wire and field [1]

ii) Z [1]; because the wire is in a continuously changing magnetic field [1]; due to a continuously changing field caused by another circuit [1]

e) Alternators: generate voltage [1]
Transformers: change voltage / current [1]; allow long distance transfer at low current [1]; to reduce energy loss due to heating of wires [1]; can step down to low voltage (for computer) [1]

10. a) i) No [1]; its source is mechanical vibration / it is high frequency sound [1]

ii) No [1]; it doesn't carry enough energy [1]

iii) Longitudinal [1]; a series of layers of compressed air, like (audible) sound [1]

b) distance = speed × time
= 1500 × (4 × 10⁻⁵) [1];
= 6 × 10⁻² or 0.06 [1];

distance to head = $\frac{\text{total distance}}{2}$ [1];
= 3 × 10⁻²m or 0.03m [1]

c) frequency = $\frac{\text{speed}}{\text{wavelength}}$
= $\frac{1500}{5 \times 10^{-4}}$
= 3 × 10⁶Hz or 3MHz [1]

d) Use sound sources such as blocks of wood banged together [1]; use reflecting surface (such as large wall) [1]; match rhythm of source with rhythm of reflections / echoes [1]; measure time for 10 repeats of sound and divide by 10 [1]; measure distance (there and back) [1]; divide distance by time [1]

e) X-rays are hazardous [1]; due to ionisation [1]

f) X-ray images are shadows [1]; use transmission (not reflection) [1]; differential absorption [1]

g) i) It uses reflections [1]; waves are (physical) vibrations (of substance/ medium) [1]

ii) It doesn't use very high frequency [1]

h) Source of waves is not created by people / technology [1]

11. a) i) Green [1]; because it is reflected most strongly / absorbed or transmitted most weakly [1]

ii) Wavelength shorter / frequency lower [1]; at violet end of spectrum [1] OR wavelength longer / frequency higher [1]; at red end of spectrum [1]

b) i) It is first transmitted [1]; then (gradually) absorbed [1]

ii) It is absorbed by the material [1]; causes (some) heating / dissipates [1]

c) i) Because of refraction [1]; due to change of speed [1]

ii) Light travels faster in air [1]; because the angle (with the normal to the surface) in air is bigger (or reverse argument) [1]

d) The range / set [1]; of different wavelengths / frequencies [1]; of the family of electromagnetic waves that travel with the same speed through space [1]

> Radio waves are not harmful to us because our bodies absorb them extremely weakly. They transfer very little energy to our bodies, either for heating or for ionisation.

e) i) The eyes detect / respond to visible light [1]

ii) There is a warming effect [1]

iii) Possible sunburn [1]

iv) ionisation effects / no noticeable sensation [1]

v) There is no (measurable) response [1]

12. a) There is more / faster energy loss from A than B [1]; A has poorer insulation [1]

b) They must replace the lost energy [1]

c) It heats the surroundings [1]; spreads thinly / dissipates [1]

d) Power [1]

e) i) and ii) **Any three sources, plus correct identification of type of resource, from:**
gas – non-renewable [2]; oil – non-renewable [2]; coal – non-renewable [2]; electricity – a mixture [2]; wood or other biofuel – renewable [2]; solar cells – renewable [2]; solar panels – renewable [2] **(1 mark for source; 1 mark for correct type)**

f) Advantages: renewable [1]; low pollution / low CO_2 emission [1]; Disadvantages: use large areas of land / not always beautiful [1]; power output not high [1]

> 25 years ago there were very few wind farms in the world. Now there are many. You need to be able to explain this change.

g) Advantages: widely available [1]; easy to transport [1]; Disadvantages: non-renewable [1]; polluting / high CO_2 emission [1]

h) More renewables [1]; primarily due to concern over climate change [1]

13. a) Arrow drawn to match the Earth's rotation [1]

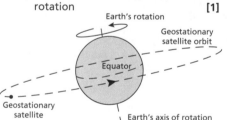

b) 24 hours (approximately) [1]

c) i) speed = $\frac{\text{distance}}{\text{time}}$ [1];
= $\frac{360\,000}{24}$ [1];
= 15 000km/h [1]

ii) = 15 000 × $\frac{1000}{3600}$ [1];
= 4.17 × 10³m/s or 4170m/s [1]

iii) There is no resistance to motion in space [1]; there is air resistance (and surface friction) on Earth [1]

d) No [1]

e) Yes [1]; its direction continually changes during one orbit, so velocity continually changes [1] [1];

f) i) The force of gravity due to the Earth [1]

ii) No **[1]**; the force is always towards the (centre of the) Earth **[1]**

g) Arrow for velocity should be perpendicular to force **[1]**; arrow for acceleration should be parallel to force and in the same direction **[1]**

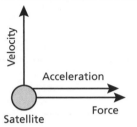

h) The Moon **[1]**

14. a) Gravity / gravitational collapse **[1]**

b) i) The number of protons / the atomic number **[1]**

ii) The number of protons + neutrons / the mass number **[1]**

c) i) Fusion / nuclear fusion **[1]**

ii) $^{2}_{1}$H has one neutron **[1]**; $^{3}_{1}$H has two neutrons **[1]**; both have one proton **[1]**

iii) In older stars, larger nuclei (or atoms) **[1]**; are made by (nuclear) fusion **[1]**

d) X = 2 **[1]**; Y = 2 **[1]**

e) i) Using the stars' spectra of electromagnetic radiation **[1]**; we can match spectral lines with those of elements on Earth **[1]**

ii) For distant galaxies **[1]**; colours in spectra have red shift **[1]**; galaxies that are further away have more red shift **[1]**

15. a) The emission **[1]**; of ionising radiation **[1]**; from substances with unstable nuclei **[1]**

b) The removal (or sometimes addition) of electrons from atoms when energy is absorbed **[1]**; which results in atoms becoming charged **[1]**

c) Gamma rays **[1]**

d) i) Alpha **[1]**

ii) Shortest tracks **[1]**

iii) It causes ionisation **[1]**; and passes energy to atoms **[1]**; of the surrounding substance **[1]**

e) Beta particles are electrons **[1]**; they are extremely small and easily change direction **[1]**; when they collide / ionise / lose energy **[1]**

Physics Equations

You must be able to recall and apply the following equations using the appropriate SI units:

Word Equation
density (kg/m^3) = $\dfrac{mass\,(kg)}{volume\,(m^3)}$
distance travelled (m) = speed (m/s) × time (s)
acceleration (m/s^2) = $\dfrac{change\ in\ velocity\,(m/s)}{time\,(s)}$
kinetic energy (J) = 0.5 × mass (kg) × (speed $(m/s))^2$
force (N) = mass (kg) × acceleration (m/s^2)
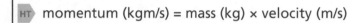 momentum (kgm/s) = mass (kg) × velocity (m/s)
work done (J) = force (N) × distance (m) (along the line of action of the force)
power (W) = $\dfrac{work\ done\,(J)}{time\,(s)}$
force exerted by a spring (N) = extension (m) × spring constant (N/m)
gravity force (N) = mass (kg) × gravitational field strength, g (N/kg)
(in a gravity field) potential energy (J) = mass (kg) × height (m) × gravitational field strength, g (N/kg)
pressure (Pa) = $\dfrac{force\ normal\ to\ a\ surface\,(N)}{area\ of\ that\ surface\,(m^2)}$
moment of a force (Nm) = force (N) × distance (m) (normal to direction of the force)
charge flow (C) = current (A) × time (s)
potential difference (V) = current (A) × resistance (Ω)
energy transferred (J) = charge (C) × potential difference (V)
power (W) = potential difference (V) × current (A) = (current $(A))^2$ × resistance (Ω)
energy transferred (J, kWh) = power (W, kW) × time (s, h)
wave speed (m/s) = frequency (Hz) × wavelength (m)
efficiency = $\dfrac{useful\ output\ energy\ transfer\,(J)}{input\ energy\ transfer\,(J)}$ × 100%

You must be able to select and apply the following equations using the appropriate SI units:

Word Equation
change in thermal energy (J) = mass (kg) × specific heat capacity (J/kg°C) × change in temperature (°C)
thermal energy for a change in state (J) = mass (kg) × specific latent heat (J/kg)
(for gases) pressure (Pa) × volume (m³) = constant (for a given mass of gas at a constant temperature)
HT pressure due to a column of liquid (Pa) = height of column (m) × density of liquid (kg/m³) × g (N/kg)
(final velocity (m/s))² − (initial velocity (m/s))² = 2 × acceleration (m/s²) × distance (m)
energy transferred in stretching (J) = 0.5 × spring constant (N/m) × (extension (m))²
HT force on a conductor (at right-angles to a magnetic field) carrying a current (N) = magnetic field strength (T) × current (A) × length (m)
HT $\dfrac{\text{potential difference across primary coil (V)}}{\text{potential difference across secondary coil (V)}} = \dfrac{\text{number of turns in primary coil}}{\text{number of turns in secondary coil}}$
potential difference across primary coil (V) × current in primary coil (A) = potential difference across secondary coil (V) × current in secondary coil (A)

Notes

Glossary and Index

Collins

OCR GCSE Revision

Physics

OCR Gateway GCSE

Workbook

Trevor Baker

Rethink Revision

Have you ever taken part in a quiz and thought *'I know this!'* but, despite frantically racking your brain, you just couldn't come up with the answer?

It's very frustrating when this happens but, in a fun situation, it doesn't really matter. However, in your GCSE exams, it will be essential that you can recall the relevant information quickly when you need to.

Most students think that revision is about making sure you **know** stuff. Of course, this is important, but it is also about becoming confident that you can **retain** that *stuff* over time and **recall** it quickly when needed.

Revision That Really Works

Experts have discovered that there are two techniques that help with all of these things and consistently produce better results in exams compared to other revision techniques.

Applying these techniques to your GCSE revision will ensure you get better results in your exams and will have all the relevant knowledge at your fingertips when you start studying for further qualifications, like AS and A Levels, or begin work.

It really isn't rocket science either – you simply need to:

- **test yourself** on each topic as many times as possible
- **leave a gap** between the test sessions.

Three Essential Revision Tips

1. **Use Your Time Wisely**

   - Allow yourself plenty of time
   - Try to start revising at least six months before your exams – it's more effective and less stressful.
   - Your revision time is precious so use it wisely – using the techniques described on this page will ensure you revise effectively and efficiently and get the best results.
   - Don't waste time re-reading the same information over and over again – it's time-consuming and not effective!

2. **Make a Plan**

   - Identify all the topics you need to revise (this All-in-One Revision & Practice book will help you)
   - Plan at least five sessions for each topic
   - One hour should be ample time to test yourself on the key ideas for a topic
   - Spread out the practice sessions for each topic – the optimum time to leave between each session is about one month but, if this isn't possible, just make the gaps as big as realistically possible.

3. **Test Yourself**

   - Methods for testing yourself include: quizzes, practice questions, flashcards, past papers, explaining a topic to someone else, etc.
   - This All-in-One Revision & Practice book provides seven practice opportunities per topic.
   - Don't worry if you get an answer wrong – provided you check what the correct answer is, you are more likely to get the same or similar questions right in future!

Visit our website to download your free flashcards, for more information about the benefits of these techniques, and for further guidance on how to plan ahead and make them work for you.

www.collins.co.uk/collinsGCSErevision

Contents

Matter, Models and Density

1 Describe the forces between the molecules in a gas.

_____ [1]

2 State the evidence that led to Rutherford claiming that the atomic nucleus was positively charged.

_____

_____ [2]

3 Explain why solid aluminium has a higher density than molten aluminium.

_____

_____ [2]

4 The density of copper is $8.96 \times 10^3 \text{kg/m}^3$.

Calculate the mass of a 2m^3 cube of copper.

Answer: _____ [2]

5 Name the particle that J. J. Thomson discovered.   Answer: _____ [1]

6 State how the Bohr model of the atom differed from Rutherford's model.

_____

_____ [2]

7 1kg of steam condenses to water at 100°C.

In the boxes below sketch how the molecules might appear in the two states.

Steam (gas)	Water (liquid)

[2]

Total Marks _____ / 12

Temperature and State

Refer to the Data Sheet on page 211 when answering these questions.

1 A small block of aluminium is given just sufficient energy to melt.

Identify **one** factor that remains unchanged when it melts.

.... [1]

2 What type of change is a change of state?

.... [2]

3 State **two** factors that are linked to the internal energy of a solid or liquid.

....

.... [2]

4 **a)** The latent heat of vaporisation of water is 2.26×10^6 J/kg.

Calculate how much energy is released if 0.1kg of steam condenses to water at 100°C.

Answer: .... [2]

b) The specific heat capacity of water is 4200J/kg/°C.

Calculate how much energy is released when 0.1kg of water at 100°C cools to 35°C.

Answer: .... [2]

c) Use your answers to parts **a)** and **b)** to explain why steam burns are more serious than burns from boiling water.

....

....

....

.... [4]

Total Marks .... / 13

Pressure

Refer to the Data Sheet on page 211 when answering these questions.

1 A teacher places a lit Bunsen burner under a can with a sealed lid, which is on a tripod.

Explain why the lid blows off the can.

....

....

.... **[3]**

2 Look at the diagram of a sealed syringe and plunger below.

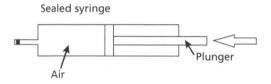

a) Explain what happens as the plunger is pushed in.

....

....

.... **[3]**

b) The pressure in the sealed syringe is 1×10^5 Pa and it has a volume of 50cm^3.

Calculate the new pressure of the air if the volume is reduced to 12.5cm^3 by pushing in the plunger. Assume that the temperature does not change.

Answer: .... **[2]**

3 An 800N man stands on a stool that has four legs.
Each leg has a cross-sectional area of 1.6×10^{-3} m^2 in contact with the ground.

Calculate the pressure exerted by the stool on the ground.

Answer: .... **[3]**

Total Marks .... / 11

Journeys

Refer to the Data Sheet on page 211 when answering these questions.

1 Describe the difference between speed and velocity.

_____

_____ [2]

2 A car travels at an average speed of 30m/s.

Calculate how far it travels in 40 seconds.

Answer: _____ [2]

3 A car travelling at 30m/s increased its speed to 70m/s in 8 seconds.

Calculate the acceleration.

Answer: _____ [2]

4 A moon is orbiting a planet in a circular orbit.

State which of the following are changing: **acceleration, velocity** or **speed**.

Answer: _____ [1]

5 A 50kg athlete is running at 8m/s.

Calculate how much kinetic energy they have.

Answer: _____ [3]

Total Marks _____ / 10

Forces

1 What is the difference between a gravitational force and an electric force?

_____

_____ [1]

2 State Newton's first law of motion.

_____

_____ [2]

3 The Earth makes a complete orbit of the Sun each year.

Describe the forces acting on the two bodies while this is happening and compare their magnitude.

_____

_____

_____

_____ [3]

4 A skydiver falling from an aircraft reaches terminal velocity.

Explain, in terms of forces, why the skydiver is not accelerating.

_____

_____

_____

_____ [3]

5 Explain what is meant by inertia.

_____ [2]

6 Explain why a satellite that is in a circular orbit around the Earth has a constant speed but changing velocity.

_____

_____ [2]

Total Marks _____ / 13

Force, Energy and Power

1 A motorcyclist and their bike have a total mass of 310kg.

Calculate their momentum when travelling at 20m/s.

Answer: .... [2]

2 When a toy water rocket at rest is pumped up, water is propelled from the bottom and it takes off.

Explain why this happens in terms of momentum.

....

....

....

.... [4]

3 Calculate how much gravitational potential energy a 60kg person gains if they climb to the top of a set of steps 12m high. (Take g to equal 10m/s².)

Answer: .... [2]

4 A machine can lift a 150kg mass 12m vertically in 90 seconds.

Calculate the power of the machine. (Take g to equal 10m/s².)

Answer: .... [2]

5 Explain why a person might find that pushing a piano is difficult, despite it having wheels.

....

.... [2]

Total Marks .... / 12

Changes of Shape

Refer to the Data Sheet on page 211 when answering these questions.

1 What is meant by a plastic material?

....

.... [1]

2 Explain why the value for gravitational field strength is larger on Jupiter than it is on Mars.

.... [1]

3 A spring extends 2cm when a force of 1N is applied.

Calculate the value of the spring constant.

Answer: .... [2]

4 A student added weights to a spring, recording the extension for each weight.
A graph was plotted of the results, as shown below.

Explain the shape of the graph.

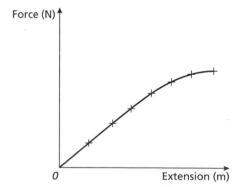

....

....

....

.... [3]

5 A spring with spring constant 80N/m is stretched 30cm.

Calculate how much energy is transferred.

Answer: .... [2]

Total Marks .... / 9

Levers, Gears and Hydraulic Systems

1 A 3m ladder is resting on a pivot at its centre point.
A 400N person sits on one side of the ladder, at a distance of 0.5m from the pivot.

Calculate the weight that would need to be placed on the other side of the ladder, at a distance of 0.8m from the pivot, to balance the person.

Answer: .... [2]

2 Car brakes use a hydraulic system to transmit pressure from the foot pedal to the brake pads on the wheels.

Explain why it is important that no air gets into the brake fluid.

....

....

....

[3]

3 The diagram below shows a hydraulic system.
A force of 10N is applied to the plunger in syringe **A**, which has a cross-sectional area of $0.2 \times 10^{-2}m^2$.
The plunger in syringe **B** has a cross-sectional area of $1.2 \times 10^{-2}m^2$.

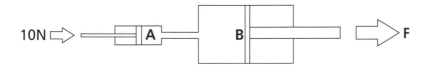

Calculate the force, **F**, that is produced on the plunger in syringe **B**.

Answer: .... [2]

Total Marks .... / 7

Electric Charge

1 What name is given to the space around a charged object in which another charged object would experience a force?

Answer: _____ [1]

2 Apart from giving a reading on an ammeter, state the **two** other detectable effects that a flow of charge can produce.

_____

_____ [2]

3 Explain why a plastic comb is an insulator, despite containing electrons.

_____ [2]

4 A battery produces a current of 5A for 10 seconds.

Calculate how much charge flows.

Answer: _____ [2]

5 A teacher rubs a plastic rod with a woollen cloth. Both the rod and cloth are insulators.

a) Explain why the plastic rod becomes positively charged and the woollen cloth becomes negatively charged.

_____

_____

_____ [3]

b) A student holds the positive rod over a discharged electroscope.

Explain why the gold leaf inside the electroscope rises.

_____

_____ [3]

Total Marks _____ / 13

Circuits

1 State what the gradient of a current–potential difference (V–I) graph represents for a component.

Answer: _____ [1]

2 A student plotted the graph below for a component in a circuit after varying the potential difference across it and measuring the current.

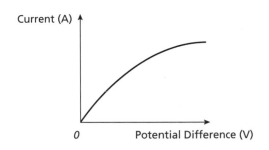

a) Suggest what the component was most likely to be.

Answer: _____ [1]

b) Explain why the graph in part **a)** has that shape for the component.

_____

_____

_____

_____

_____ [4]

3 A student obtained the graph below by varying the potential difference across a component and measuring the current.

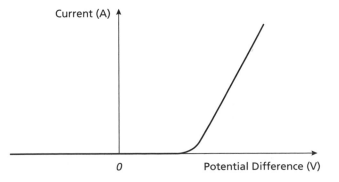

a) Name the component.

Answer: _____ [1]

b) State what the graph indicates about the current direction.

_____ [1]

Total Marks _____ / 8

Resistors and Energy Transfers

1 Calculate the value of the potential difference across **V** in the circuit below.

Answer: _____ [2]

2 Calculate the combined resistance of the two parallel resistors below.

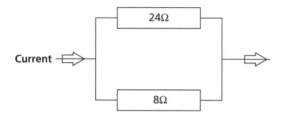

Answer: _____ [2]

3 Explain why connecting resistors in parallel makes the combination behave like a single resistor of a lower value than either of the individual resistors.

_____

_____

_____

_____

[4]

4 A 2Ω, a 3Ω and a 5Ω resistor are connected in series with a 20V battery.

Calculate the current that flows through them.

Answer: _____ [2]

Total Marks _____ / 10

Magnetic Fields and Motors

Refer to the Data Sheet on page 211 when answering these questions.

1 A compass is placed near a coil of wire that is connected via a closed switch to a 12V battery.
After 15 seconds, the switch is opened.
The compass needle moves and points in a different direction.

Suggest a reason for this.

_____

_____

_____ [2]

2 A student investigates the magnetic field due to a coil placed on a piece of paper and
connected to a 6V battery.
They sprinkle iron filings around the coil.

a) Suggest how they would identify the strongest region of the magnetic field.

_____

_____ [1]

b) What difference would the student have noticed if the same experiment had been
carried out with a 20V battery rather than a 6V one? Explain your answer.

_____

_____ [3]

3 A wire of length 0.5m is placed in a magnetic field of magnetic flux density 2.4×10^{-2}T.

Calculate the force that acts on the wire if a current of 3A flows in it.

Answer: _____ [2]

Total Marks _____ / 8

Electromagnetism

Refer to the Data Sheet on page 211 when answering these questions.

1 Describe how the output current from an alternator differs from that of a dynamo when connected to a circuit.

[2]

2 Explain how an alternator produces an output current when connected to a lamp.

[4]

3 A magnet is placed inside a coil that is connected in a circuit to an ammeter.

Explain why removing the magnet causes a current to flow, and how this opposes the removal of the magnet.

[3]

4 A transformer has 30 turns in the primary coil and 360 in the secondary coil.

a) Calculate the output potential difference in the secondary coil if an 8V alternating supply were connected to the primary coil.

Answer: _____ [2]

b) Name this type of transformer.　　　　Answer: _____ [1]

Total Marks _____ / 12

Sound, Sonar and Ultrasound

1 What type of wave is a sound wave?   Answer: _____ [1]

2 An electric bell is ringing loudly inside a sealed bell jar, that is connected to a pump.
   When the air has been pumped out, the bell continues to vibrate but cannot now be heard.

   Explain why this happens.

   _____

   _____

   _____

   _____ [2]

3 A student stands a distance from a wall and claps their hands.
   When they hear the echo, they clap again.
   They keep this going in a regular rhythm while another student measures the time between claps.

   a) Suggest how the speed of sound could be calculated using this data.

   _____

   _____ [2]

   b) Explain why it would have been better to measure the time for 10 claps.

   _____

   _____

   _____ [2]

4 A person standing on a platform at a station first hears the sound of the train through
   the rails.
   A few seconds later, they hear the train approaching in the air.

   Suggest why they hear it through the air later.

   _____

   _____ [2]

Total Marks _____ / 9

Electromagnetic Radiation

1 A pebble is dropped into a ripple tank, producing a water wave. This can model an electromagnetic wave.

State what property of the wave cannot now be changed.

Answer: _____ [1]

2 A dentist will leave the room when a patient is having an X-ray.

Suggest the reason for this.

_____ [2]

3 Explain how X-rays are used at a hospital to check for fractures in the body.

_____

_____

_____

_____ [3]

4 A radio station broadcasts by using radio waves of wavelength 1500m.
The speed of electromagnetic radiation is 3×10^8 m/s.

Calculate the frequency of the station.

Answer: _____ [3]

5 Multiple sclerosis is a condition that leads to poor circulation and lower temperatures in the extremes of the body, such as the hands.

Identify the part of the electromagnetic spectrum that could be used by a scanner to detect this condition.

Answer: _____ [1]

6 X-rays and gamma rays are forms of ionising radiation.

Describe how they can affect the body.

_____

_____ [2]

Total Marks _____ / 12

Waves at Surfaces and Inside Materials

1 What term is used to explain why the bottom of a swimming pool appears closer than it really is?

Answer: _____ [1]

2 State the **two** wave properties that change when waves from a red light source pass from air into glass.

_____ [2]

3 The lens that is used in a magnifying glass is fatter in the middle than at the outside. What type of lens is this?

Answer: _____ [1]

4 Complete this ray diagram for a concave lens.

[4]

5 A student shines a red light source onto a red and blue striped scarf in a dark room.

State the colour(s) that the scarf will appear to be and explain why.

_____

_____

_____ [3]

6 When white light shines onto a prism at a certain angle, a coloured spectrum is produced.

Explain why the colours are separated in this way.

_____

_____

_____ [3]

Total Marks _____ / 14

Nuclei of Atoms

1. Name the particles that are found in an atomic nucleus.

   _____ [2]

2. Uranium atoms, atomic number 92, can be found with different numbers of neutrons.

   What word describes these different forms of the same element?

   Answer: _____ [1]

3. Gamma rays are known as ionising radiation.

   Describe how they can affect atoms.

   _____

   _____ [2]

4. A teacher puts different absorbers between a radioactive source and a Geiger counter.
   When paper is used, the count rate on the Geiger counter doesn't change.
   However, the count rate drops when aluminium is used and drops further when lead is used.

   Name the types of radiation that the source emitted.

   _____ [2]

5. State the values for **X** and **Y** in the equation for radioactive decay below.

   $^{235}_{92}U = ^{Y}_{X}Th + ^{4}_{2}He$

   _____ [2]

6. Two nuclei of carbon have different numbers of neutrons.

   $^{12}_{6}C$ $^{14}_{6}C$

   a) Describe the structure of each nucleus.

   _____

   _____ [2]

   b) State the charge on each nucleus.

   _____ [1]

   Total Marks _____ / 12

Decay, Fission and Fusion

1 Explain what is meant by the term 'half-life'.

_____

_____ [1]

2 A sample of radioactive iodine, with a mass of 64g and a half-life of 13 hours, was left to decay.

a) Calculate the amount of iodine that was left after 52 hours.

Answer: _____ [3]

b) Calculate the fraction of the starting nuclei that remained after 52 hours.

Answer: _____ [1]

3 Explain what is meant by the term 'irradiation'.

_____ [1]

4 Below is a diagram of a smoke detector.
It uses americium-241, with a half-life of 432 years, which emits alpha particles.
The detector sounds an alarm if electrons, released due to ionisation, do not reach it.

a) Explain how the presence of smoke particles would set off the alarm.

_____

_____ [2]

b) Suggest why it is useful that americium-241 has a long half-life.

_____

_____ [2]

Total Marks _____ / 10

Systems and Transfers

Refer to the Data Sheet on page 211 when answering these questions.

1 A hot saucepan is dropped into a sink full of cold water.

   a) Explain why the saucepan cools down.

   _____

   _____ [2]

   b) Describe what happens to the cold water as a result.

   _____ [1]

2 According to the principle of conservation of energy: 'the total energy of the system remains the same, whatever happens inside the system'.

   State **two** things that could change the energy of the system.

   _____

   _____ [2]

3 Calculate the amount of heat required from an electric kettle to raise the temperature of 1.2kg of water from 20°C to boiling point at 100°C.
   (Take the specific heat capacity of water to be 4200J/kg/°C.)

   Answer: _____ [2]

4 A farm has a hydroelectric system to produce electrical power from a generator.
   20kg of water falls 15m down a vertical hillside every second.

   a) State the main energy changes that take place in the system.

   _____

   _____ [3]

   b) In reality, energy will be lost from the system. State what form that energy is likely to take.

   Answer: _____ [1]

   Total Marks _____ / 11

Energy, Power and Efficiency

1 When charging a mobile phone from the mains, not all the electrical energy is transferred through the transformer (charger).

Describe how energy is 'lost'.

_____ [1]

2 Energy used up by large electrical items is measured in kilowatt-hours. What is a kilowatt-hour?

_____ [2]

3 State **two** ways in which the heating of a house can be improved by reducing heat loss.

_____

_____ [2]

4 A 250V mains fan draws a current of 2A from the power supply.

  a) Calculate the power of the fan.

                           Answer: _____ [2]

  b) Calculate how much energy the fan will draw from the mains power supply if it is on for 10 minutes.

                           Answer: _____ [2]

5 A 250V mains kettle draws a current of 8A from a power supply to heat 2kg of water. It takes 400 seconds to raise the temperature of the water by 70°C in order for it to boil. (The specific heat capacity of water = 4200J/kg/°C.)

  a) Calculate the power of the kettle.

                           Answer: _____ [2]

  b) Calculate how much energy it would supply in 400 seconds.

                           Answer: _____ [2]

Total Marks _____ / 13

Physics on the Road

1 State **two** distances that determine the total stopping distance of a car when the driver needs to brake suddenly.

[2]

2 **a)** A car travelling at a velocity of 25m/s is brought to rest in 10 seconds.

Calculate the deceleration.

Answer: _____ [2]

b) The car has a mass of 1500kg. Calculate what force would have acted to cause the deceleration.

Answer: _____ [2]

3 Two students carry out an experiment to measure their reaction time.
They use a metre ruler and a stopwatch.
They found the following equation useful:

$$\text{reaction time} = \frac{\sqrt{2 \times \text{distance (metres)}}}{g}$$

a) Describe how they could carry out the experiment.

[6]

b) Suggest what would be a sensible result for their reaction time.

[1]

Total Marks _____ / 13

Energy for the World

1 Explain what is meant by a non-renewable energy source.

....

.... [2]

2 A steam engine uses coal as a fuel.

   a) Describe the energy changes that take place in the engine as it moves along the track.

....

....

.... [4]

   b) Alcohol is a renewable bio-fuel that can be produced from crops on farms.
       It could be used to run steam engines by burning it in a boiler.

       Suggest **two** reasons why this wouldn't be a good idea.

....

....

.... [2]

3 Nuclear power stations use uranium-235 as a fuel.
   Uranium-235 has a long half-life of 7×10^8 years.

   a) Suggest why uranium is considered to be a non-renewable fuel.

....

.... [1]

   b) State **one** advantage and **one** disadvantage of using nuclear power.

....

....

.... [2]

Total Marks .... / 11

Energy at Home

Refer to the Data Sheet on page 211 when answering these questions.

1 What is the difference between an a.c. supply and a d.c. supply?

_____

_____ [2]

2 State the potential difference and frequency of the mains electricity supply.

_____ [2]

3 A teacher sets up a model electricity transmission system.
A diagram of the apparatus, showing the number of turns in each coil of the transformer, is shown below.

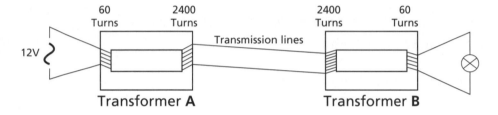

a) State what type of transformer is represented by Transformer **B**.

_____ [1]

b) Calculate the potential difference across the transmission lines.

Answer: _____ [2]

c) Calculate the current in the transmission lines if the 12V a.c. power supply delivered a current of 2A.

Answer: _____ [3]

Total Marks _____ / 10

Space

1 A moon is travelling in a circular orbit around a planet.

Explain why the moon's velocity changes but its speed does not.

_____

_____ [2]

2 Explain the evidence from the light from distant galaxies that can be used to support the Big Bang theory.

_____

_____

_____

_____ [4]

3 An enormous cloud of dust and hydrogen was pulled together by the force of gravity to form our star, the Sun.

a) Explain how this caused nuclear fusion, which powers the Sun.

_____

_____

_____ [3]

b) Explain why the Sun doesn't collapse under the force of gravity.

_____

_____ [2]

4 Geostationary satellites are artificial satellites used for global communications.

Explain why they are called 'geostationary'.

_____

_____ [2]

Total Marks _____ / 13

Notes

Collins

GCSE (9–1)
Physics
Paper 1 (Higher Tier)

Time allowed: 1 hour 45 minutes

You must have:

- the Data Sheet (page 211)

You may use:

- a scientific calculator
- a ruler

Instructions

- Use black ink. You may use a HB pencil for graphs and diagrams.
- Answer **all** the questions.
- Write your answer to each question in the space provided.
- Additional paper may be used if required.

Information

- There are **90** marks available on this paper.
- The marks for each question are shown in brackets [ ].
- Quality of extended response will be assessed in questions marked with an asterisk (*).

SECTION A

Answer **all** the questions.

You should spend a maximum of 30 minutes on this section.

1 Identify which of these liquids has the lowest density.

A

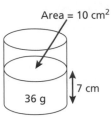

Area = 10 cm²

7 cm

36 g

B

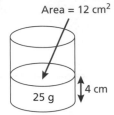

Area = 12 cm²

4 cm

25 g

C

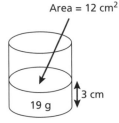

Area = 12 cm²

3 cm

19 g

D

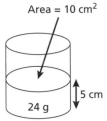

Area = 10 cm²

5 cm

24 g

Your answer ☐ [1]

2 A balloon containing helium is released from a fairground.

As it rises, it expands, the mass remaining constant.

In the fairground

Volume = 4000 cm³

High above the fairground

Volume = 5000 cm³

The density of helium, measured in the balloon, high above the fairground was found to be 0.14 kg/m³.

Calculate the density of the helium in the balloon in the fairground.

A 0.130 kg/m³

B 0.175 kg/m³

C 0.182 kg/m³

D 0.112 kg/m³

Your answer ☐ [1]

3 A metal sphere has a volume of 4×10^{-5} m³.
Its density is 8.0×10^3 kg/m³.

Calculate its mass.

A 2.0×10^8 kg

B 0.5×10^{-8} kg

C 3.2×10^{-1} kg

D 3.2×10^{-2} kg   Your answer ☐ **[1]**

4 Which of the following measurements is a good approximation for the size of an atom?

A 1×10^{-11} m

B 1×10^{-10} m

C 1×10^{-9} m

D 1×10^{-6} m   Your answer ☐ **[1]**

5 Compasses are used to plot the magnetic field lines between two permanent magnets, with identical but opposing north poles (see below).

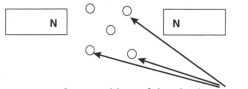

Some positions of the plotting compasses

Identify which of the following is the correct plot for the magnetic field in this case.

Your answer ☐ **[1]**

Turn over

6   A wire is connected to a battery and an open switch.

Part of the wire **XY** is placed between opposite poles of a magnet.

That part of the wire **XY** is free to move.

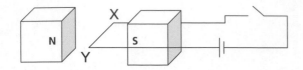

Identify the direction in which the wire will move when the switch is closed.

A 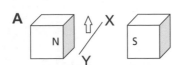   B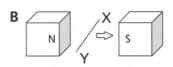

C 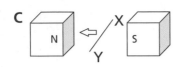   D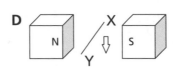

Your answer ☐ **[1]**

7   A conductor of length 0.5 m, carrying a current of 2.0 A is placed in a magnetic field of strength 2.0×10^{-2} T.

Calculate the force that acts on the conductor.

Use the following equation:

force on a conductor carrying a current = magnetic field strength × current × length

A 2.0×10^{-2} N

B 0.5×10^{-2} N

C 4.0×10^{-2} N

D 20×10^{-2} N

Your answer ☐ **[1]**

8 A toy truck of mass 6 kg is travelling at 0.4 m/s along a track.

It collides with another truck of mass 4 kg that is travelling in the same direction at 0.2 m/s, as shown in the diagram.

They stick together after the collision. *v* is the velocity of both trucks stuck together.

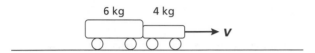

Identify which of the following is the correct value of *v*.

A 0.30 m/s

B 0.60 m/s

C 0.24 m/s

D 0.32 m/s   Your answer [ ]   **[1]**

9 A train travels 240 km in 3 hours.

Calculate how long it would take to travel 80 km at half the speed.

A 2 hours

B 6 hours

C 1 hour

D 4 hours   Your answer [ ]   **[1]**

10 A person has to apply a force of 20 N in order to lift a 40 N load using a 20 N beam balanced on a pivot, as shown below.

The pivot is 0.6 m from the load.

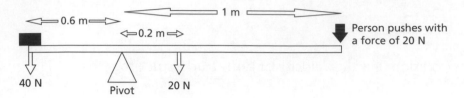

Which of the following is the correct value for the clockwise moment around the pivot?

A 20 Nm

B 240 Nm

C 24 Nm

D 60 Nm

Your answer ☐ [1]

11 A suspended spring, of spring constant 12 N/m, is stretched 40 cm when a load is added.

Calculate how much work is done.

Use the formula:
energy transferred in stretching = 0.5 × spring constant × (extension)^2

A 480 J

B 2.4 J

C 1.92 J

D 0.96 J

Your answer ☐ [1]

12 Identify the correct value for the resistance of resistor **R** in the circuit below.

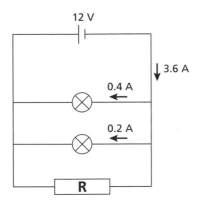

A 3.33 Ω

B 30.00 Ω

C 4.00 Ω

D 20.00 Ω

Your answer ☐ **[1]**

13 A student induces a current by moving a bar magnet in and out of the coil.
The north pole of the magnet faces the coil, as shown below.
The a.c. ammeter indicates when a current is flowing.

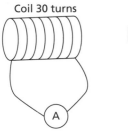

Identify which change would increase the current in the coil.

A Turning the magnet round so that the south pole faces the coil

B Moving the magnet more quickly in and out of the coil

C Having fewer turns of wire on the coil

D Using a thinner wire in the coil

Your answer ☐ **[1]**

Turn over

14 Look at the diagram below.

Gear **X** is rotated clockwise at 1.0 rotations per second.

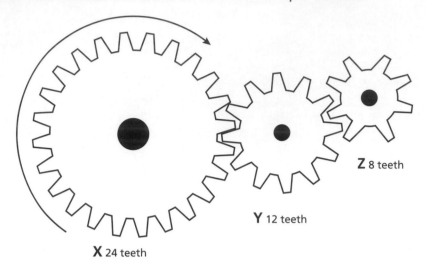

Z 8 teeth

Y 12 teeth

X 24 teeth

Which row in the table is the correct description of the movement of gear Z?

	Direction of rotation	Rotations per second
A	anticlockwise	3
B	clockwise	3
C	anticlockwise	1.5
D	clockwise	1.5

Your answer ☐ [1]

15 A 12 Ω resistor has a current of 2 A flowing through it.

Which of the following is the correct power of the resistor?

A 48 W

B 6 W

C 288 W

D 24 W

Your answer ☐ [1]

SECTION B

Answer **all** the questions.

16 A student sets up the apparatus below to measure the specific latent heat of ice.

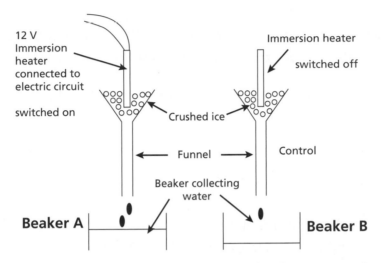

12 V Immersion heater connected to electric circuit

switched on

Immersion heater

switched off

Crushed ice

Funnel

Control

Beaker collecting water

Beaker A

Beaker B

(a) Sketch a circuit diagram, including an ammeter and voltmeter, to show how the immersion heater should be connected to the 12 V supply so that the power of the immersion heater can be calculated.

[2]

(b) Suggest extra apparatus that might be needed and the measurements that should be taken to successfully calculate the specific latent heat of ice.

[4]

Turn over

(c) Explain why the student set up a control experiment.

....

.... **[1]**

(d) The student repeats the experiment five times to have more confidence in the conclusion. One of the calculations gives too high a value for the specific latent heat of ice.

Suggest one error in measurement that might have caused this.

....

.... **[1]**

(e) In the experiment, 0.1 kg of ice melted.
The specific latent heat of fusion of ice = 3.34×10^5 J/kg.

Calculate how much energy is required from the heater to produce this change in state.

Use the following equation:
energy = mass × specific latent heat of fusion of ice

Answer: .... J **[2]**

17 A toy submarine is allowed to sink in a tank of sunflower oil.
    The density of sunflower oil is 0.92 kg/m³.
    The distance from the surface to points **A** (0.5 m),
    B (2 m) and **C** (4 m) are shown on the diagram.

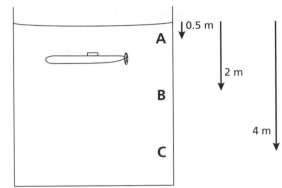

(a) Using the formula given below, calculate the pressure due to the sunflower oil on the submarine at point **C**.

   pressure due to a column of liquid = height of the column × density of the liquid × g

   Answer: .... Pa   **[2]**

(b) Explain why this would not be the true value of the pressure at point **C**.

   ....

   ....   **[1]**

(c) Calculate how much the pressure changes as the submarine rises from point **C** to point **A**.

   Answer: .... Pa   **[3]**

(d) Use the molecular model to explain why the sunflower oil has a higher density than the air above the surface.

   ....

   ....

   ....

   ....   **[2]**

Turn over

18 A student is investigating how a step-up transformer works.

They can change the number of turns on the secondary coil only.

They set up the transformer as shown below. The wires used are insulated.

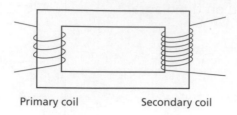

Primary coil   Secondary coil

(a) Explain why the transformer shown is a step-up transformer.

....

....

....

.... [2]

(b) On the transformer below, complete the circuit diagrams that the student would need to use in order to investigate the following formula:

$$\frac{\text{potential difference across primary coil (V)}}{\text{potential difference across secondary coil (V)}} = \frac{\text{number of turns in primary coil}}{\text{number of turns in secondary coil}}$$

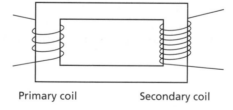

Primary coil   Secondary coil   [2]

(c) Describe how the student should carry out the investigation.

....

....

....

....

....

.... [4]

(d) Explain why the student must use only a very low input voltage for this experiment.

....

.... **[1]**

(e) The student connects the transformer to an alternating input potential difference of 6 V.
The transformer now has 30 turns in the primary coil and 120 turns in the secondary coil.

Calculate the potential difference (voltage) that would be measured across the output of the secondary coil.

Answer: V   **[2]**

(f) The student then changes the input to a 6 V battery.

Calculate the output voltage.

Answer: V   **[1]**

Turn over

19 In an experiment, trolley **X** with mass 0.5 kg is travelling along a horizontal track at a constant speed of 12 m/s.

It collides with a stationary trolley **Y** of identical mass.
The two trolleys stick together after the collision and travel horizontally along the track.

The graph below shows the motion of trolley **X**.

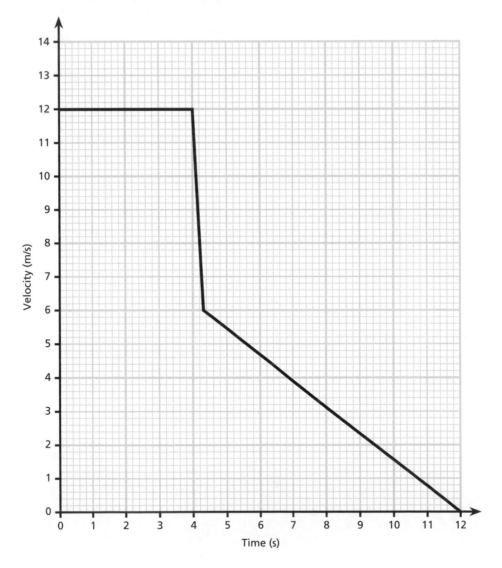

(a) Calculate the distance travelled by trolley **X** in the first 3 seconds.

Answer: _____ m   **[1]**

(b) (i) Calculate the deceleration that occurred when the two trolleys stuck together.

Answer: _____ m/s² **[2]**

(ii) Calculate the force acting on the two trolleys that caused the deceleration.

Answer: _____ N **[2]**

(c) Calculate the total momentum of the two trolleys after 7.5 seconds.

Answer: _____ kg m/s **[2]**

(d) On the grid below, sketch the velocity against time graph for trolley **Y** during the experiment. **[2]**

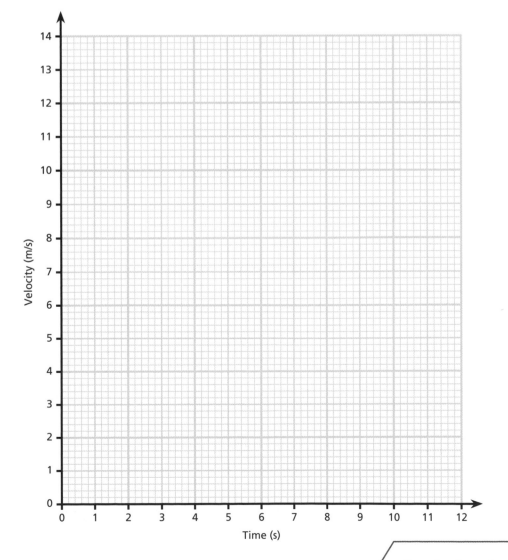

Turn over

20 A student is investigating the behaviour of a thermistor.
They set up the circuit shown here.

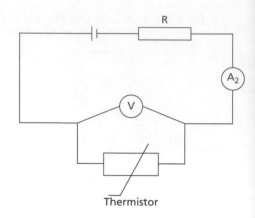

(a) The student was given a kettle, two thermometers, two beakers and some crushed ice.

Explain how the student could use this apparatus to demonstrate the behaviour of a thermistor at different temperatures.

....

....

....

....

....   **[4]**

(b) The student replaced the voltmeter with a multimeter to directly record the resistance of the thermistor at different temperatures.

The results were recorded in the table below.

Temperature (°C)	Resistance (kΩ)			
	Reading 1	Reading 2	Reading 3	Mean
0	28.1	28.1	28.2	28.1
10	20.4	20.3	20.2	20.3
20	14.1	14.3	14.1	14.2
30	11.1	11.1	11.2	11.1
40	8.9	9.1	9.2	9.1
50	7.9	9.1	7.9	7.9
60	7.1	7.2	7.1	7.1
70	6.6	6.5	6.4	6.5
80	6.1	5.9	5.9	5.9
90	5.5	5.4	5.5	5.5

(i) There is an anomaly in the table of results.

Identify the anomaly and explain how the student should deal with it.

....

....

.... **[2]**

(ii) Write down a conclusion you can you draw from the table of results.

....

.... **[1]**

(c) The student then connected up the following circuit.
The same thermistor was used.

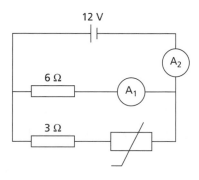

(i) Calculate the reading on ammeter A$_2$ if the thermistor has a resistance of 9 Ω.

Answer: .... A **[2]**

(ii) The thermistor is placed in a beaker of ice.

Describe what difference, if any, the student would notice on the ammeter readings.

....

.... **[1]**

Turn over

21 **(a)** A student rubs a plastic comb with a woollen cloth. The comb becomes positively charged.

(i) Explain how the comb becomes charged.

....

.... [2]

(ii) Suggest a way to show that the comb is charged.

....

.... [2]

(iii) For your suggestion in part **(ii)** what would you expect to see and why?

....

.... [2]

(b) A charged metal sphere is resting on an insulated base.
A wire is connected to an ammeter and a metal water pipe.
The student touches the sphere with the other end of the wire.
A charge flows as shown below.

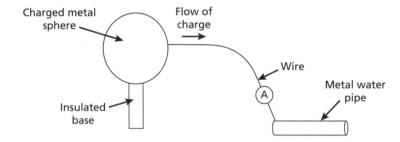

(i) The ammeter registers 30 mA initially.
The student suggests that a current of 30 mA flowed in the wire for 20 seconds.

Calculate the quantity of charge that the student thought flowed in that time.
Include the units in your answer.

Answer: .... [2]

(ii) Give **one** reason why the student was wrong to assume that the current of
30 mA flowed for 20 seconds.

.... [1]

22   In an experiment, a spring was suspended vertically from a horizontal beam.
     Marked weights, 1 N each, were attached to the bottom of the spring, one at a time.
     A metre rule was used to measure the extension when each weight was added.

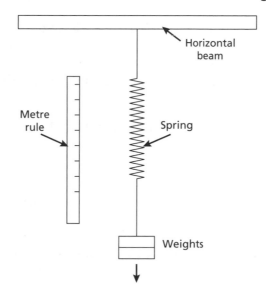

The results were recorded in the table below.

Force (N)	Extension (cm)
1	1.6
2	3.2
3	4.8
4	6.4
5	8.1
6	9.6
7	11.2
8	12.8
9	14.4
10	15.9
11	19.7
12	28.1

(a) Use the data to describe the relationship between force and extension for the spring when
       the weight was increased from 1 N to 10 N.

_____

_____ **[1]**

Turn over

(b) Calculate the spring constant for the spring using the extension when 4 N was the weight.

Answer: _____ N **[2]**

(c) Calculate how much work was done when the spring was stretched by the 4 N weight. Use the formula:

energy transferred in stretching = 0.5 × spring constant × (extension)^2

Answer: _____ J **[2]**

(d) Suggest why the extension does not follow the same relationship once the weight exceeds 11 N.

_____

_____ **[1]**

(e) (i) If astronauts had carried out the experiment with the same spring and the same marked weights on the surface of the Moon, describe how the table of results would differ from the one above.

_____

_____ **[1]**

(ii) Explain your answer to part **(i)** ($g = 1.6$ m/s^2 on the Moon's surface).

_____

_____ **[1]**

23   A student is investigating how the resistance of a wire varies with length.
      They set up the following circuit. A metre rule was placed along side the wire.

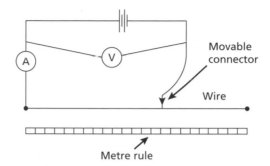

(a) Explain why the reading on the voltmeter remained constant throughout the experiment.

....

.... **[1]**

(b) The student used an 18 V battery and obtained the following results:

Resistance (Ω)	Length of wire (cm)
25	100
22	90
18	75
15	60
12	50
10	40
9	30
8.5	20

(i) Calculate the current that flowed when the wire was 50 cm.

Answer: .... A **[3]**

(ii) Calculate the rate of thermal energy transfer from the wire when it was 30 cm long.

Answer: .... W **[2]**

Turn over

(c) The student plotted a graph of their results.

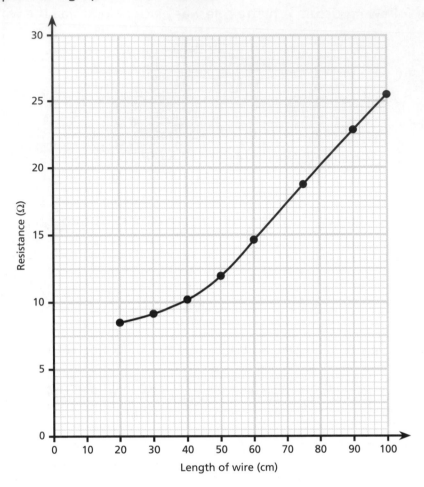

(i) What is the value of the resistance when the wire was 58 cm long?

Answer: _____ Ω **[1]**

(ii) The graph is linear when the wire is between 50 and 100 cm long.

Explain why it is curved between 20 and 40 cm long.

_____

_____

_____ **[2]**

END OF QUESTION PAPER

Collins

GCSE (9–1)
Physics
Paper 2 (Higher Tier)

H

Time allowed: 1 hour 45 minutes

You must have:

- the Data Sheet (page 211)

You may use:

- a scientific calculator
- a ruler

Instructions

- Use black ink. You may use a HB pencil for graphs and diagrams.
- Answer **all** the questions.
- Write your answer to each question in the space provided.
- Additional paper may be used if required.

Information

- There are **90** marks available on this paper.
- The marks for each question are shown in brackets [ ].
- Quality of extended response will be assessed in questions marked with an asterisk (*).

SECTION A

Answer **all** the questions.

You should spend a maximum of 30 minutes on this section.

1   Radium-88 is a radioactive element that decays to radon by emitting an alpha particle.
The equation is shown below.

$$^{226}_{88}Ra \longrightarrow ^{X}_{Y}Rn + ^{4}_{2}He$$

Identify which are the correct values of **X** and **Y**.

	X	Y
A	226	89
B	88	227
C	222	86
D	86	222

Your answer ☐ [1]

2   A driver is travelling at 30 m/s in a car on a test track.
The driver has to carry out an emergency stop.
The thinking distance and braking distances are measured.

Which statement is **true** if there had been three more people in the car?

A   The braking distance would be larger.

B   The thinking distance would be larger.

C   The overall stopping distance would remain the same.

D   The braking distance would remain the same.

Your answer ☐ [1]

3 The diagram below shows light waves passing from air into a glass at an angle to the surface. Refraction occurs.

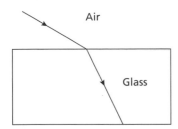

Which of the following is true about the light waves refracted in this example?

	Velocity	Frequency	Wavelength
A	unchanged	increases	decreases
B	decreases	decreases	unchanged
C	unchanged	decreases	increases
D	decreases	unchanged	decreases

Your answer ☐ [1]

4 Sunlight shining on a solar cell has a power of 1000 W/m^2.
The solar cell is 20% efficient and has an area of 0.5 m^2.

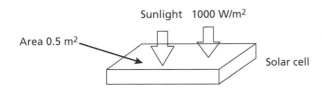

How much electrical energy would the solar cell produce per second?

A 80 J

B 800 J

C 400 J

D 100 J

Your answer ☐ [1]

Turn over

5   A boat sends out a sonar signal from a sonar echo device.
     Four seconds later the echo is detected.
     The water is 3000 m deep.

Sonar echo device

Sonar

3000 m

Which is the correct speed of sound in water?

A   750 m/s

B   375 m/s

C   1500 m/s

D   300 m/s   Your answer [ ]   [1]

6   A car is involved in an accident.
     The driver is wearing a seatbelt.
     An airbag inflates on the steering wheel during the accident.

     Which of the following statements is **not** correct about how to reduce the force acting on the
     driver during the accident?

     A   A longer accident time causes a smaller force on the body of the driver.

     B   The seatbelt stretches by a small amount, increasing the accident time.

     C   The seatbelt keeps the driver's body firmly in the seat, reducing the force.

     D   The airbag compresses as the driver's body moves forward.   Your answer [ ]   [1]

7 Which of the following statements is **not** true about the Solar System?

  A Asteroids and comets have circular orbits around the Sun.

  B Neptune has more moons than Mars.

  C Mercury takes a shorter time to orbit the Sun than Venus does.

  D The Moon is a natural satellite of the Earth.   Your answer ☐ **[1]**

8 In an experiment a signal generator is connected to a loudspeaker.
A microphone connected to an oscilloscope is placed in front of the loudspeaker,
as shown below.

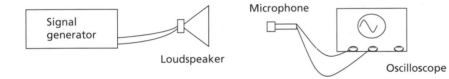

Traces on the oscilloscope, obtained for two different settings on the signal generator,
are shown below.

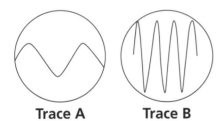

  Trace A   **Trace B**

Identify which of the following have changed from trace **A** to trace **B**.

  A Only the amplitude has increased.

  B The amplitude and frequency have increased.

  C Only the frequency has increased.

  D The amplitude has increased but the frequency has decreased.   Your answer ☐ **[1]**

9 Protactinium-233 has a half-life of 27 days.

A 64 g sample of the element is left in a cupboard.

How much protactinium would remain after 108 days?

A 16 g

B 4 g

C 8 g

D 32 g   Your answer [ ] **[1]**

10 A radioactive source emits two types of radiation.

The paths of the particles passing through an electric field were tracked and shown below.

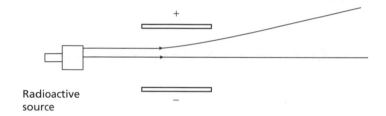

Radioactive
source

Identify the types of radiation shown in the diagram.

A Beta particles and gamma rays

B Alpha particles and beta particles

C Alpha particles and gamma rays

D Beta particles and protons   Your answer [ ] **[1]**

11 A 250 V mains hair drier draws a current of 10 A from the supply.

How much energy would it use if it were switched on for 2 minutes?

A 2500 J

B 5000 J

C 3×10^5 J

D 3×10^4 J

Your answer [   ] **[1]**

12 A ball bearing is dropped from rest in a vacuum.

Which graph shows how the velocity varies with time?

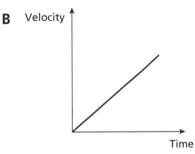
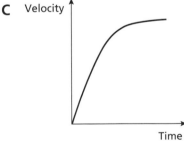
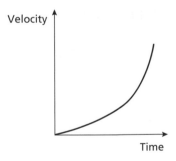

Your answer [   ] **[1]**

Turn over

13 Which of the following statements is **false**?

    A Infrared cameras are used to show up heat loss from houses.

    B Gamma rays, X-rays and ultraviolet are types of ionising radiation.

    C Satellites use microwaves for communication.

    D Ultraviolet has a longer wavelength than microwaves.   Your answer ☐ **[1]**

14 The Earth is travelling in orbit around the Sun.

Identify which statement is **true** about the Earth.

    A The Earth is pulling on the Sun only.

    B The Earth is accelerating.

    C The velocity of the Earth is constant.

    D The speed of the Earth is changing due to the force of gravity.   Your answer ☐ **[1]**

15 A seismometer is used to detect seismic waves from an earthquake.

An earthquake occurs on the opposite side of the world to a seismometer.

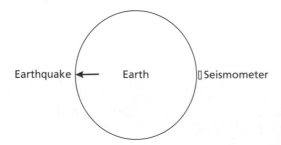

Which of the following statements is **true** about the seismometer?

    A Only P-waves will be detected.

    B Only S-waves will be detected.

    C No waves will reach the seismometer.

    D Both P-waves and S-waves will be detected.   Your answer ☐ **[1]**

SECTION B

Answer **all** the questions

16 Maxine, who is a teacher, uses a Geiger counter to measure the activity (rate of decay) of a radioactive source.

The results are recorded and a graph plotted using them, as shown below.

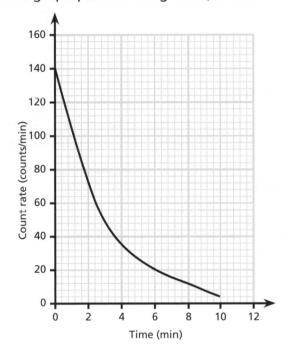

(a) (i) Use the graph to determine the half-life of the source.

Answer: _____ min **[2]**

(ii) Suggest why, although there is a clear decay curve, not all of the points are on the curved line of best fit.

_____

_____

_____

_____

[2]

Turn over

(b) Maxine now uses another radioactive source.

She places different absorbers between the radioactive source and the Geiger counter, as shown below.

The counts per minute are recorded on the Geiger counter for each absorber.

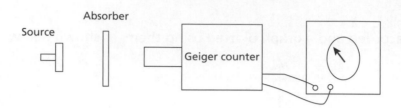

Maxine records her results in the table.

Absorber	Count rate (counts/min)
None	160
Paper	158
Aluminium	48
Lead	15

(i) Identify the types of radiation emitted from the source.

.... **[2]**

(ii) Explain why there was still a reading with lead as the absorber.

.... **[1]**

(iii) Radiation is dangerous.

Describe how Maxine should carry out this experiment safely.

....

....

.... **[2]**

17   A teacher was demonstrating waves by shaking a slinky.
     The pattern is shown below.

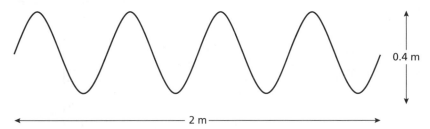

     The frequency of the wave was 2 Hz.

(a) What type of wave is the teacher demonstrating?

                                        Answer: .... **[1]**

(b) (i) State the amplitude of the wave.

                                        Answer: .... m **[1]**

   (ii) State how the amplitude relates to energy.

     ....

     .... **[2]**

   (iii) Using the diagram above, calculate the speed of this wave.

                                        Answer: .... m/s **[3]**

Turn over

(c) A white light source is used to shine light through a prism.
A spectrum is seen on the white screen.

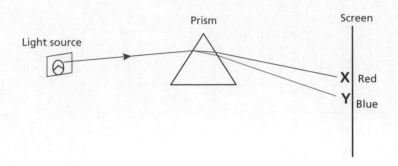

(i) Explain why a coloured spectrum is seen on the white screen.

....

....

....

.... **[3]**

(ii) State what would be seen on the screen at point **Y** if a red filter were put in
front of the light source.

....

.... **[1]**

18 A seismometer records the signal from an earthquake.
    Both P-waves and S-waves are detected, as shown below.
    The seismometer was 2400 km away from the earthquake.

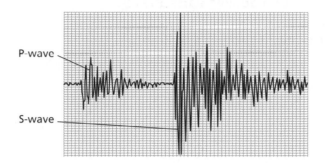

(a) State which wave has the greatest amplitude.

Answer: .... [1]

(b) What type of wave is a P-wave?

Answer: .... [1]

(c) Both types of seismic wave are detected by the seismometer and both come from
    the same earthquake.

    Based on these facts, state the conclusion that can be drawn about the structure
    of the Earth between the two points.
    Explain your answer.

    ....

    .... [2]

(d) The P-wave travels at a velocity of 8000 m/s and the S-wave travels at 3000 m/s.

    Calculate how long each wave took to travel from the earthquake to the seismometer.

Answer: .... s [5]

Turn over

(e) Some regions of the world are under threat from earthquakes.

The cities lie near geological fault lines.

New buildings have dampers fitted near their bases.

These offer some protection against earthquakes.

Suggest how dampers might protect a building.

....

.... **[1]**

19 The Hubble telescope is a large telescope in space.

It travels in orbit at 8.05 kilometres per second around the Earth at a height of 547 kilometres.

The power of the Sun falling on Hubble is 1368 W/m².

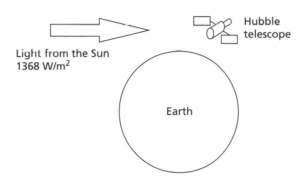

Light from the Sun
1368 W/m²

Hubble
telescope

Earth

(a) State the advantages of the telescope being above the atmosphere when viewing the emissions of all wavelengths from distant galaxies.

....

....

.... **[3]**

(b) Give **two** disadvantages of having a telescope in space.

....

.... **[2]**

(c) Hubble's solar panels produce 300 W/m² of power.

Calculate their efficiency.

Answer: .... % **[3]**

Turn over

(d) When viewing light from two different galaxies **X** and **Y**, two different spectra were obtained.

They were compared with the normal visible spectrum, shown below.

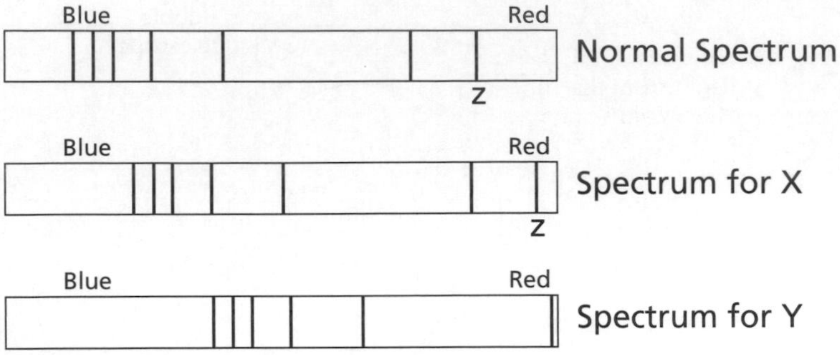

Blue   Red   Normal Spectrum

Z

Blue   Red   Spectrum for X

Z

Blue   Red   Spectrum for Y

(i) State the conclusions that can be made about Galaxies **X** and **Y** from the spectra.

....

.... **[2]**

(ii) Suggest why the spectral line **Z** doesn't appear in the spectrum for Galaxy **Y**. Explain your answer.

....

....

.... **[2]**

20 **(a)** Toni is investigating suitable insulators for her house.

She puts water at 100 °C into an insulated copper can.

She measures and records the temperature every minute for 10 minutes.

There are several different insulators available.

Toni's results are shown in the table below.

Time (min)	Temperature (°C)
0	100
1	90
2	78
3	68
4	60
5	55
6	49
7	45
8	42
9	38
10	35

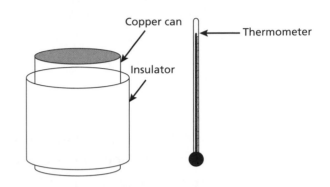

(i) Plot the readings on the graph below.

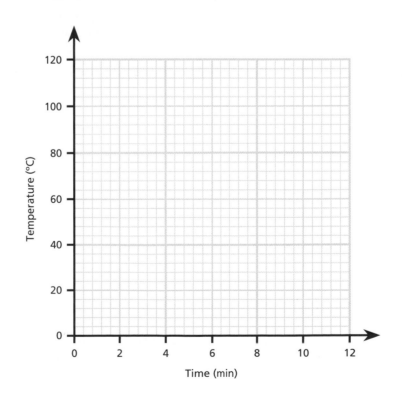

[2]

Turn over

(ii) Estimate from your graph what the temperature would have been after 11 minutes.

.... **[1]**

(iii) Describe how Toni should complete her experiment to conclude which is the best insulator.

....

....

.... **[2]**

(b) There are heat losses in a power station.
Below is diagram showing these heat losses.
They are calculated for every 100 joules stored in the coal.

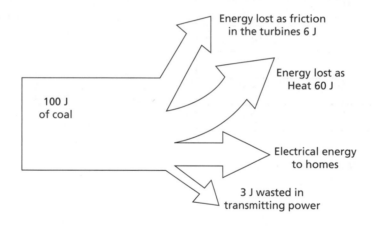

(i) Calculate how much electrical energy reaches the homes for every 100 joules of coal in this power station.

Answer: .... J per 100J of coal **[2]**

(ii) Calculate the efficiency of this power station.

Answer: .... % **[2]**

21 A circuit was set up, as shown below, to transmit energy over a long distance.

(a) Suggest why the lamp was very dim.

....

.... **[1]**

(b) The circuit was then modified, as shown below, by adding two transformers.

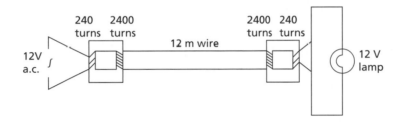

(i) Explain why the battery was replaced by an alternating supply.

....

.... **[1]**

(ii) Explain why the lamp now shines brightly.

....

.... **[2]**

c) $\dfrac{\text{potential difference across primary coil}}{\text{potential difference across secondary coil}} = \dfrac{\text{number of turns in the primary coil}}{\text{number of turns in the secondary coil}}$

(i) Using the formula above, calculate the potential difference across the 12 m wire.

Answer: .... V **[2]**

Turn over

(ii) Calculate the current that would flow in the 12 m wire if the current from the 12 V supply were 2 A.

Answer: .... A   **[2]**

(iii) State the assumption you have made in your calculations above.

....

....   **[1]**

22 A model wind turbine is being tested.

A fan is used to generate the wind.

An anemometer is used to measure the wind speed.

As the blades rotate, they drive a dynamo, producing a potential difference.

A resistor is connected with the dynamo, as shown below.

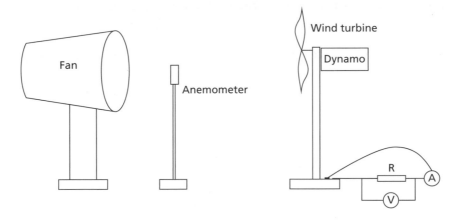

The power of the turbine, generated from the dynamo, was determined from the current through the resistor and the potential difference across it.

(a) From the results a graph was plotted of power output against wind speed.

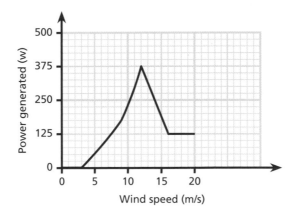

   (i) State the wind speed at which the output power was at its maximum value.

Answer: .... **[1]**

  (ii) If the wind speed is too high, friction in the dynamo or vibrations in the blades of the turbine can cause energy losses.

State between which wind speeds the output power was falling. **[2]**

(iii) State **one** disadvantage of using this type of wind turbine to power a 375 W floodlight on a remote farm.

_____ **[1]**

(b) Solar panels are used by some farmers rather than wind turbines.

  (i) Suggest **two** advantages of using solar panels to generate electricity rather than fossil fuels.

_____

_____

_____ **[2]**

  (ii) State **two** reasons a farmer might decide not to install solar panels on their farm.

_____

_____

_____ **[2]**

23 A 60 kg driver is travelling in a car at 12 m/s.

A child runs out from the curb and the driver has to do an emergency stop.

The graph below shows the changes in the car's velocity.

It covers the time from when the driver first saw the child ($t = 0$).

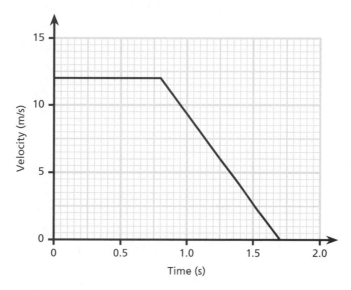

(a) Calculate the distance (thinking distance) that the driver covered before applying the brakes.

Answer: _____ m **[2]**

(b) Calculate the deceleration of the driver once the brakes were applied.

Answer: _____ m/s² **[2]**

(c) Suggest **one** factor that might have increased the braking distance.

_____

_____ **[1]**

Turn over

(d) The graph on the facing page showed the thinking and braking distances for an alert driver.

Sketch a graph below to show how it would have appeared had the driver been under the influence of alcohol or very tired.

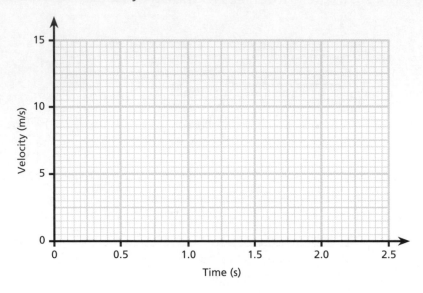

[2]

END OF QUESTIONS

Data Sheet

change in thermal energy = m × specific heat capacity × change in temperature

thermal energy for a change in state = m × specific latent heat

for gases : pressure × volume = constant (for a given mass of gas and at a constant temperature)

$(\text{final velocity})^2 - (\text{initial velocity})^2 = 2 \times \text{acceleration} \times \text{distance}$

energy transferred in stretching = $0.5 \times \text{spring constant} \times (\text{extension})^2$

potential difference across primary coil × current in primary coil =
potential difference across secondary coil × current in secondary coil

HT **pressure due to a column of liquid = height of column × density of liquid × g**

HT **force on a conductor (at right-angles to a magnetic field) carrying a current =
magnetic flux density × current × length**

HT $$\frac{\text{potential difference across primary coil}}{\text{potential difference across secondary coil}} = \frac{\text{number of turns in primary coil}}{\text{number of turns in secondary coil}}$$

Answers

Page 140 – Matter, Models and Density

1. The forces are weak **[1]**
2. The nucleus repelled **[1]**; positive alpha particles **[1]**
3. The aluminium atoms are more closely packed in the solid form (than when in the liquid state) **[1]**; so the density is higher **[1]**
4. mass = density × volume, mass = $(8.96 \times 10^3) \times 2$ **[1]**; $= 1.792 \times 10^4$kg **[1]** (Accept 17 920kg)
5. The electron **[1]**
6. Bohr's model had the electrons in orbits **[1]**; around the nucleus **[1]**
7. A correct sketch of molecules in steam **[1]**; and water **[1]**

Steam (gas)   Water (liquid)

Page 141 – Temperature and State

1. **Any one from:** temperature **[1]**; mass **[1]**; the number of aluminium atoms **[1]**; the structure of aluminium atoms **[1]**
2. A reversible **[1]**; physical change **[1]**
3. The forces between the solid / liquid's atoms or molecules **[1]**; the motion of the atoms or molecules **[1]**
4. a) Energy = $0.1 \times (2.26 \times 10^6$J) **[1]**; $= 2.26 \times 10^5$J **[1]** (Accept 226 000J or 226kJ)
   b) Heat = $0.1 \times 4200 \times 65$ **[1]**; $= 2.73 \times 10^4$J **[1]** (Accept 27 300J or 27.3kJ)

   > The change in temperature is 100 – 35 = 65°C. You need to use this value in your calculation.

   c) There is greater energy from steam changing state to water than boiling water cooling **[1]**; when steam comes in contact with skin, both energies are added together **[1]**; as the change of state and cooling both take place **[1]**; and greater energy release to the skin causes greater damage **[1]**

Page 142 – Pressure

1. As the air inside the can heats up, the molecules move faster (Accept gain kinetic energy) **[1]**; the force on the walls and lid increases **[1]**; causing an increase in the pressure and the lid to blow off **[1]**
2. a) As the plunger is pushed in, the volume of the air decreases **[1]**; leading to more collisions between the air molecules and the walls of the syringe **[1]**; causing an increase in air pressure inside the syringe **[1]**
   b) $P_1V_1 = P_2V_2$,
   so $\dfrac{(1 \times 10^5) \times 50}{10^6} = \dfrac{P_2 \times 12.5}{10^6}$ **[1]**;
   $P_2 = 4 \times 10^5$Pa **[1]** (Accept 400 000Pa)

   > Here each volume in cm³ is converted is to m³ by dividing by 10^6. (1m = 100cm, so 1m³ = $100 \times 100 \times 100 = 1 000 000$cm³ or 10^6cm³.) But the 10^6 denominators cancel in the calculation. (The ratio of the volumes in cm³ is the same as the ratio of volumes in m³.)

3. Total area of the stool legs = $4 \times (1.6 \times 10^{-3}) = 6.4 \times 10^{-3}$m² **[1]**;
   Pressure = $\dfrac{\text{force}}{\text{area}} = \dfrac{800}{6.4 \times 10^{-3}}$ **[1]**;
   $= 1.25 \times 10^5$Pa **[1]** (Accept 125 000Pa or Nm⁻² as the units)

Page 143 – Journeys

1. Speed is a scalar quantity as it only has magnitude **[1]**; velocity is a vector as it has both magnitude and direction **[1]**
2. Distance = average speed × time **[1]**; distance = 30 × 40 = 1200 m **[1]**
3. Acceleration = $\dfrac{\text{change in velocity}}{\text{time}}$
   $= \dfrac{(70 - 30)}{8}$ **[1]**; $= 5$m/s² **[1]**
4. Velocity and acceleration **[1]**

   > An object on a circular path is constantly changing direction, so acceleration and velocity also change because they are vector quantities involving direction.

5. KE = $\frac{1}{2}mv^2$ **[1]**; $= 0.5 \times 50 \times 8^2$ **[1]**; $= 1600$J **[1]**

Page 144 – Forces

1. A gravitational force can only be attractive; an electrical force can be repulsive or attractive **[1]**
2. A body stays still or keeps moving at constant velocity **[1]**; unless an external force acts on it **[1]**

3. There is an attractive force from the Sun pulling on the Earth **[1]**; there is also an attractive force from the Earth pulling on the Sun **[1]**; these forces are equal in magnitude but opposite in direction **[1]**
4. At terminal velocity, the force of gravity downwards (weight) is balanced by air friction (resistive force) **[1]**; producing an equal and opposite upward force **[1]**; so no net force is acting / the resultant force is zero **[1]**
5. Inertia is a measure of how difficult it is **[1]**; to change the velocity of an object **[1]**
6. The satellite is constantly changing direction in orbit, so the velocity (a vector quantity) is changing **[1]**; speed (a scalar quantity) doesn't depend on direction **[1]**

Page 145 – Force, Energy and Power

1. Momentum = 310kg × 20m/s **[1]**; $= 6.2 \times 10^3$kg m/s **[1]**
2. Momentum is conserved **[1]**; the total momentum of the rocket and water is zero when the rocket is at rest **[1]**; the water leaving the rocket has momentum in a downwards direction **[1]**; so the rocket must have an equal momentum in the opposite direction **[1]**
3. Potential energy = 60 × 10 × 12 **[1]**; $= 7200$J **[1]**
4. Power = $\dfrac{150 \times 10 \times 12}{90}$ **[1]**; $= 200$W **[1]**
5. The work done by the person has to overcome friction **[1]**; as well as to move the piano **[1]**

Page 146 – Changes of Shape

1. A material that is deformed when a force is applied and does not return to its original shape when the force is removed **[1]**
2. Jupiter has greater mass than Mars **[1]**
3. spring constant = $\dfrac{\text{force}}{\text{extension}} = \dfrac{1}{2 \times 10^{-2}}$ **[1]**; $= 50$N/m **[1]**

   > You must be able to recall the following equation and rearrange it to make the spring constant the subject:
   > force = spring constant × extension

4. The straight line part of the graph shows the spring obeying Hooke's law and behaving elastically **[1]**; the point at which the graph just stops showing proportionality (begins to curve) is the elastic limit **[1]**; after that point, the graph curves, showing plastic behaviour **[1]**

5. Energy = 0.5 × spring constant × (extension)² = 0.5 × 80 × (30 × 10⁻²)² **[1]**; = 3.6J **[1]**

Page 147 – Levers, Gears and Hydraulic Systems

1. 400 × 0.5 = weight × 0.8 **[1]**; weight = 250N **[1]**

> sum of clockwise moments = sum of anticlockwise moments

2. When pressure is applied, air gets compressed (because it is a gas) **[1]**; whereas the liquid brake fluid does not **[1]**; this would lead to a reduction in the pressure being transmitted to the brake pads **[1]**

3. $\frac{10}{0.2 \times 10^{-2}} = \frac{force}{1.2 \times 10^{-2}}$ **[1]**; force = 60N **[1]**

> pressure at A = pressure at B

Page 148 – Electric Charge

1. An electric field **[1]**
2. A magnetic field **[1]**; and heat **[1]** (Accept produces light)
3. The electrons are not free to move **[1]**; so charge cannot flow **[1]**
4. charge = current × time = 5 × 10 **[1]**; = 50C **[1]**
5. a) Electrons are transferred from the rod to the cloth **[1]**; having lost electrons, the rod is now positively charged **[1]**; having gained electrons, the cloth is now negatively charged **[1]**
   b) Electrons are attracted up to the plate at the top **[1]**; leaving both the stem and gold leaf positively charged **[1]**; the leaf is repelled by the stem and rises **[1]**

Page 149 – Circuits

1. Resistance **[1]**
2. a) A (filament) light bulb / lamp **[1]**
   b) The graph is linear for low values of current and obeys Ohm's law **[1]**; then as the current increases, the graph becomes non-linear as the wire in the bulb (lamp) heats up **[1]**; this increases the resistance **[1]**; due to more collisions between the moving electrons and (increasingly) vibrating metal atoms **[1]**
3. a) A diode **[1]**
   b) Current can only flow one way through it **[1]**

Page 150 – Resistors and Energy Transfers

1. *Either* ratio of resistors is 12 : 4 = 3 : 1 **[1]**; as potential difference has the same ratio, potential difference = $\frac{36}{3}$ = 12V **[1]**

   Or using $I = \frac{V}{R}$

   current flowing = $\frac{36}{12}$ = 3A, so

   potential difference across 4Ω resistor = 3 × 4 **[1]**; = 12V **[1]**
2. $\frac{1}{R} = \frac{1}{24} + \frac{1}{8}$ **[1]**; $R = 6\Omega$ **[1]**
3. The current has two paths to flow through the combination **[1]**; and the potential difference is the same for each path **[1]**; so the total current flowing into the combination is greater than for each individual branch **[1]**; consequently the combined resistance for the combination is lower than for each separate branch **[1]**

> $V = IR$. V is constant so if I increases, as it does with two parallel branches, then R must decrease.

4. Total resistance = 2 + 3 + 5 **[1]**; $V = IR$: 20 = current × 10, current = 2A **[1]**

Page 151 – Magnetic Fields and Motors

1. The compass needle is no longer affected by the magnetic field of the coil, as no current is flowing through the wires of the coil **[1]**; therefore, the needle moves to point towards the Earth's magnetic south pole **[1]**
2. a) There will be a greater density of iron filings (in the strongest region of the magnetic field) **[1]**
   b) The field lines would appear closer together **[1]**; as a greater current is flowing in the coil **[1]**; strengthening the magnetic field **[1]**
3. force = 2.4 × 10⁻² × 3 × 0.5 **[1]**; = 3.6 × 10⁻²N **[1]**

Page 152 – Electromagnetism

1. The output current from an alternator is a.c. (alternating current) **[1]**; whereas from a dynamo it is d.c. (direct current) **[1]**
2. As the coil rotates through 360°, the wires cut the magnetic field lines, firstly when going up **[1]**; then in the opposite direction when going down **[1]**; this induces a current first in one direction in the wire **[1]**; and then in the opposite direction, creating an alternating current **[1]**
3. Moving the magnet produces a changing magnetic field through the coil **[1]**; this causes a current to be induced in the coil **[1]**; the direction of the induced current is such that it creates a magnetic field that opposes that of the magnet (and so attracts it) **[1]** (Accept a similar argument about a magnetic field being produced to oppose the change made by moving the magnet, from an induced current)
4. a) Ratio of the number of turns = ratio of the potential differences,

   $\frac{30}{360} = \frac{8}{V_s}$ **[1]**; secondary potential difference, V_s = 96V **[1]**
   b) Step-up transformer **[1]**

Page 153 – Sound, Sonar and Ultrasound

1. A longitudinal wave **[1]**
2. Sound needs particles in order for the vibration to be passed on **[1]**; once the air has been removed the bell is in a vacuum, and the sound can't travel as there are no particles to transfer the vibration **[1]**
3. a) Measure the distance to the wall and double it **[1]**; then divide that number by the time between the claps to get the speed of sound **[1]** (Accept a correct answer written as an equation, i.e. speed of sound = $\frac{\text{distance to wall} \times 2}{\text{time between claps}}$
   b) Dividing the time for 10 claps by 10 gives a more precise value for the time the sound took to reflect **[1]**; because the error is divided by 10 **[1]** (1 mark only for just saying it is more precise; a reason must be given for the second mark)

> The error in starting and stopping a stopwatch is the same whether timing 1 clap or 10 claps.

4. Sound travels faster in solids than gases **[1]**; the molecules are more closely packed in solids and so transfer energy more quickly **[1]**

Page 154 – Electromagnetic Radiation

1. Frequency **[1]**
2. The dentist takes many X-rays in a day **[1]**; the risk to the health of the dentist is high **[1]**
3. X-rays pass through the body tissue **[1]**; but are absorbed by bones **[1]**; any crack or gap in the bones would lead to some X-rays in that region reaching the detector, giving an image of the fracture **[1]**
4. speed = frequency × wavelength **[1]**; frequency = $\frac{3 \times 10^8}{1500}$ **[1]**; = 2 × 10⁵Hz **[1]** (Accept 200 000Hz)
5. Infrared **[1]**
6. If absorbed by cells of the body **[1]**; they ionise atoms and can cause chemical changes that can be harmful **[1]** (Accept they can cause cells to become cancerous)

Page 155 – Waves at Surfaces and Inside Materials

1. Refraction **[1]**
2. Wavelength **[1]**; and speed (velocity) **[1]**
3. A convex lens **[1]**
4. A correct diagram showing internal refraction **[1]**; and three correct emerging rays showing divergence **[3]**

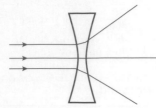

5. The scarf will appear to be red and black [1]; the red sections will reflect red light and the blue sections will absorb the red light, appearing black [1]; as there is no blue light to reflect [1]

6. Each colour has a different wavelength [1]; the speed of the coloured light in the prism depends on the wavelength [1]; the prism refracts each wavelength through a different angle (producing a spectrum) [1]

Page 156 – Nuclei of Atoms

1. Protons [1]; and neutrons [1]
2. Isotopes [1]
3. Ionising radiation can cause atoms to lose electrons [1]; and become ions [1]
4. Beta particles [1]; and gamma rays [1]
5. X = 90 [1]; Y = 231 [1]
6. a) Both have six protons [1]; but the carbon-12 nucleus has six neutrons and the carbon-14 has eight neutrons [1]
   b) The charge on both nuclei is the same, +6 [1]

Page 157 – Decay, Fission and Fusion

1. Half-life is the time taken for the number of radioactive nuclei in a sample to halve [1]
2. a) 52 hours is 4 half-lives [1]; 64g halved 4 times (64 → 32 → 16 → 8 → 4) [1]; = 4g [1]
   b) $\frac{4}{64} = \frac{1}{16}$ [1]
3. Irradiation is the exposure of an object to ionising radiation [1]
4. a) Smoke particles would block the alpha particles, stopping ionisation [1]; no electrons would be produced to flow to the detector [1]
   b) It doesn't need to be handled or replaced [1]; so avoids exposure to alpha particles [1]

Page 158 – Systems and Transfers

1. a) Energy in the form of heat [1]; is transferred from the saucepan to the water [1]
   b) The water warms up as it gains energy [1]
2. The system gains energy from outside (by heating or work done on it) [1]; or loses energy to the outside (by transferring heat or doing work) [1]
3. Heat = 1.2 × 4200 × 80J [1]; = 4.032 × 10^5 J [1] (Accept 403 200J)
4. a) Gravitational potential energy [1]; changes to kinetic energy [1];

which changes to electrical energy [1]
   b) Heat / thermal [1]

Page 159 – Energy, Power and Efficiency

1. It is transferred in the form of thermal energy in the transformer [1]
2. A kilowatt-hour is the energy that a 1 kilowatt appliance transfers [1]; in 1 hour [1]
3. **Any two from:** reduce air flow between the inside and outside of the house [1]; insulate the loft [1]; use double glazing [1]; use carpets [1] (Accept any other sensible suggestion)
4. a) power = 250 × 2 [1]; = 500W [1]
   b) energy = 500 × 10 × 60 [1]; = 3 × 10^5 J [1] (Accept 300 000J)
5. a) power = 250 × 8 [1]; = 2000W [1]
   b) energy = 2000 × 400 [1]; = 8.0 × 10^5 J [1] (Accept 800 000J)

Page 160 – Physics on the Road

1. Thinking distance [1]; and braking distance [1]
2. a) acceleration (deceleration) = $\frac{\text{change in velocity}}{\text{time}} = \frac{25}{10}$ [1]; = 2.5m/s² [1]
   b) force = 1500 × 2.5N [1]; = 3750N [1]
3. a) One student holds the ruler vertically [1]; the other puts their open hand level with the 0cm mark, so that the ruler is between their fingers and thumb [1]; the student drops the ruler [1]; the other student catches it [1]; the length at which the ruler was caught is recorded [1]; the reaction time is calculated [1]
   b) Any value between 0.15 and 0.3 seconds [1]

Page 161 – Energy for the World

1. A non-renewable energy source is one that once it is used cannot be replaced [1]; in a reasonable time scale [1] (Accept: A natural resource that cannot be grown or produced [1]; at the same time as it is consumed [1])
2. a) Stored chemical energy (in coal) [1]; changes to heat in the boiler [1]; which produces steam [1]; which gives the engine kinetic energy [1]
   b) **Any two from:** burning alcohol still emits carbon dioxide [1]; alcohol is highly flammable so it is a hazard to people near the engine [1]; if farms produce alcohol, it would reduce the number of fields for food production [1]; there would be difficulty in transporting it, either by road or on the train [1]; extra emissions would be a factor with transportation [1] (Accept any other sensible response)

3. a) The amount of uranium in rocks on Earth is decreasing because of its decay [1]
   b) **Any one advantage from:** it doesn't emit carbon dioxide or particulates into the atmosphere [1]; a small amount of fuel produces an enormous quantity of energy [1] (Accept any similar sensible response)
   Any one disadvantage from: waste products are radioactive and dangerous [1]; waste products need to be transported for reprocessing [1]; radioactive waste is problematic to dispose of [1]; radioactive waste has a long half-life so will remain dangerous for hundreds of years [1] (Accept any similar sensible response)

Page 162 – Energy at Home

1. An a.c. supply produces a current that keeps rapidly changing direction [1]; the current from a d.c. supply only goes one way [1]
2. 230V [1] (Accept 240V or 250V); 50Hz frequency [1]
3. a) A step-down transformer [1]
   b) $\frac{12}{V_s} = \frac{60}{2400}$ [1]; $V_s = \frac{12 \times 2400}{60} = 480V$ [1]
   c) In transformer A, power in = power out [1]; 12 × 2 = 480 × current in transmission lines [1]; current = 0.05A [1]

> Transformers are almost 100% efficient.

Page 163 – Space

1. The moon has a constant speed because it travels in a circular path with a constant radius / always covers the same distance in the same time [1]; the velocity changes because the force of gravity on the satellite means that the direction of travel constantly changes [1]

> Speed is a scalar quantity and velocity is a vector quantity.

2. Light coming from stars in distant galaxies is red-shifted [1]; the further away a galaxy is, the more red-shifted the light [1]; the more red shift, the faster the galaxy is moving away from us [1]; this happens in all directions, like the result of an explosion [1].
3. a) As the gas and dust are compressed, they get extremely hot [1]; the high temperature and pressure sets off nuclear fusion of smaller nuclei of atoms into bigger ones [1]; this releases enormous quantities of energy [1]

b) The heat produced from the fusion process causes expansion **[1]**; which counterbalances the gravitational forces **[1]**

4. They are geostationary because they appear to remain stationary in space **[1]**; above the same point on the Earth's surface **[1]**

Pages 165–186 – Exam Practice Paper 1

Section A

1. D   **[1]**
2. B   **[1]**
3. C   **[1]**
4. B   **[1]**
5. D   **[1]**
6. D   **[1]**
7. A   **[1]**
8. D   **[1]**
9. A   **[1]**
10. C   **[1]**
11. D   **[1]**
12. C   **[1]**
13. B   **[1]**
14. B   **[1]**
15. A   **[1]**

Section B

16. **a)** A circuit drawn with a battery, ammeter in series **[1]**; and a voltmeter connected in parallel to the heater/ battery, as shown **[1]** (or similar arrangement)

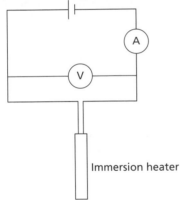

Immersion heater

b) Apparatus: balance to measure the mass of the water collected (accept a measuring cylinder to calculate mass from the volume if known density of water is referred to, but not on its own) **[1]**; stopwatch to measure the time the heater was on **[1]**
Measurements: mass of water collected due to the immersion heater (by subtracting the mass in the control beaker B from the mass collected in beaker A) **[1]**; time the heater was on **[1]**

c) To measure the mass of ice that melted due to the room temperature and not due to the heater **[1]**

d) Too low a measurement of the mass of water collected or too high a reading of the time the

heater was on **[1]**

e) energy = $0.1 \times (3.34 \times 10^5)$ **[1]**; 3.34×10^4J **[1]** (Accept 33 400J)

17. **a)** pressure = $4 \times 0.92 \times 10$ **[1]**; = 36.8Pa **[1]**

b) Atmospheric pressure needs to be added **[1]**

c) pressure at A = $0.5 \times 0.92 \times 10$ = 4.6Pa **[1]**; pressure change = 36.8 – 4.6 **[1]**; = 32.2Pa **[1]**

d) Sunflower oil is a liquid so its molecules are close together; air is a mixture of gases so its molecules are far apart **[1]**. So sunflower oil has a higher density because there are more molecules per m³ **[1]**

18. **a)** There are more turns in the secondary coil than in the primary coil **[1]**; therefore there is a higher potential difference across the secondary coil than across the primary coil **[1]**

b) The circuit should be drawn to include an alternating supply **[1]**; and a voltmeter in parallel to each of the coils **[1]**

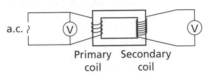

Primary   Secondary
coil   coil

c) Measure and record the number of turns on the primary coil (constant value) and the number of turns on the secondary coil **[1]**; measure and record the potential difference across the primary and secondary coils **[1]**; change, measure and record the number of turns on the secondary coil – for each value measure and record the potential difference across the primary and secondary coils **[1]**; analyse the results to see if they agree with the formula (or similar explanation) **[1]**

d) Because the transformer will step up the voltage and could give a dangerously high output voltage **[1]**

e) $\dfrac{V\text{(primary)}}{V\text{(secondary)}} = \dfrac{\text{turns (primary)}}{\text{turns (secondary)}}$,

$\dfrac{6}{V\text{(secondary)}} = \dfrac{30}{120}$,

V (secondary) = 24V **[2]**

f) 0V **[1]**

> There is no output potential difference as transformers only work on an alternating supply.

19. **a)** From the graph: distance travelled = 12m/s × 3s = 36m **[1]**

b) i) deceleration = $\dfrac{6-0}{12-4.3}$ **[1]**; = 0.78m/s² **[1]**
(Accept acceleration = –0.78m/s²)

ii) force = 1 × 0.78 **[1]**; = 0.78N **[1]**
(Accept force = –0.78 N)

c) Taken from graph: velocity after 7.5s = 3.5m/s **[1]**; total momentum = 3.5kgm/s **[1]**

d) Line drawn to show v = 0 from 0 to 4 seconds, with a steep gradient rising to v = 6 between 4 and 4.3 seconds **[1]**; line falling from v = 6 to v = 0 between 4.3 seconds and 12 seconds **[1]**

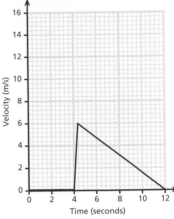

20. **a)** Pour hot water in one beaker and put crushed ice in another, place a thermometer in each beaker **[1]**; lower the thermistor into each beaker in turn, measure and record the temperature and the corresponding readings on the voltmeter and ammeter **[1]**; keep the thermometer and the thermistor in the beaker of hot water and repeat the measurements as the water cools **[1]**; the resistance at each temperature can now be calculated and a conclusion drawn **[1]**

b) i) The 'reading 2' at 50°C is too high at 9.1Ω **[1]**; ignore the anomaly and just use the other two readings to calculate the average resistance at 50°C OR repeat the faulty measurement of resistance at 50°C **[1]**

ii) An inverse relationship: as the temperature of the thermistor rises, its resistance decreases **[1]**

c) i) 3A (2A through the 6Ω resistor, 1A through the 12Ω of the 3Ω resistor plus thermistor) **[2]**

ii) Reading on A_1 is unchanged, reading on A_2 decreases **[1]**

21. **a) i)** Electrons are transferred from the comb to the woollen cloth when it is rubbed **[1]**; removal of electrons results in the comb becoming positively charged **[1]**

ii) Comb held near a running tap **[1]**; will attract the water **[1]** OR comb brought near an uncharged electroscope **[1]**; will cause the leaf to rise **[1]** OR comb will pick up small pieces of paper or attract hair **[1]**; if held over it **[1]** (Accept any other similar suggestion)

iii) Mention of opposite charges attracting, like charges repelling **[1]**; the explanation must include a mention of electrostatic induction **[1]**

b) i) charge = current × time [1]; =
$\frac{30}{1000}$ × 20 = 0.6 coulombs [1]

ii) **Any one from:** the potential difference decreased as charge flowed off the sphere [1]; the current flowing would decrease with time [1]; the current would not be constant [1] (or similar answer based on current falling with time) [1]

22. a) Force is proportional to extension / the relationship is linear **[1]**

b) force = spring constant × extension,
4 = spring constant × 0.064 [1]; spring constant = 62.5N/m [1]

c) Energy transferred = ½kx²
= 0.5 × 62.5 × (0.064)² [1];
= 0.128J (Accept 0.13J) [1]

d) The elastic limit of the spring has been exceeded **[1]**

e) i) For each marked weight the extension would be less **[1]**

ii) The true weight of each marked weight would in reality be less, as the acceleration due to gravity is less on the Moon's surface than on Earth (or similar explanation) **[1]**

23. a) The voltmeter measured the potential difference of the battery **[1]**

b) i) Correct identification that resistance = 12Ω when the wire is 50cm long [1]; $V = IR$, 18 = I × 12 [1]; I =1.5A [1]

ii) Current at 30cm = $\frac{18}{9}$ = 2A [1]; power = VI = 18 × 2 = 36W [1]

c) i) 14Ω [1]

ii) A shorter wire heats up more because it has a lower resistance, leading to a higher current flowing [1]; the heat increases the vibration of the atoms in the wire, leading to more collisions with the moving electrons, which means the resistance is greater than for a cold wire [1]

Pages 187–210 Exam Practice Paper 2

Section A
1. C [1]
2. A [1]
3. D [1]
4. D [1]
5. C [1]
6. C [1]
7. A [1]
8. B [1]
9. B [1]
10. A [1]
11. C [1]
12. B [1]
13. D [1]
14. B [1]
15. A [1]

Section B
16. a) i) From the graph in 2.1 minutes the count rate drops from 140 to 70, then 70 to 35 in 2.1 minutes [1]; 2.1 minutes [1] **(Accept 2 minutes)**

ii) Decay is a random process for each nucleus (giving slight variations in counts/min) [1]; there are so many nuclei that overall there is a pattern [1]

b) i) Beta [1]; and gamma [1]

ii) The background count (due to natural radiation in the environment) [1]

iii) **Any two from:** without handling the source (using forceps) [1]; keeping as much distance from the source as possible [1]; using the source for a minimum time [1]

17. a) Transverse waves [1]

b) i) $\frac{0.4}{2}$ = 0.2m [1]

ii) The greater the amplitude, the greater the amount of energy [1]; the wave is carrying [1]

iii) wavelength = $\frac{2m}{4 \text{ waves}}$ = 0.5m [1]; speed = frequency × wavelength [1]; = 2 × 0.5 = 1m/s [1]

c) i) White light is made up of all the colours [1]; each colour has a different wavelength (accept frequency) [1]; each wavelength (frequency) is refracted through a different angle by the prism, producing the spectrum [1]

ii) No colour / no light [1]

A red filter absorbs blue light – it **doesn't** replace it with red. There is no light from the source now reaching the screen at point Y.

18. a) The S-wave [1]

b) Longitudinal [1]

c) There is no liquid rock between the earthquake region and the seismometer [1]; S-waves cannot travel through liquids [1]

d) velocity = $\frac{\text{distance}}{\text{time}}$, so time = $\frac{\text{distance}}{\text{velocity}}$ [1]; time for P-wave = $\frac{2400 \times 10^3 \text{m}}{8000\text{m/s}}$ [1]; = 300 s [1]; time for S-wave = $\frac{2400 \times 10^3 \text{m}}{3000\text{m/s}}$ [1]; = 800 s [1]

e) Dampers absorb the energy from the seismic waves (preventing some of the energy from reaching the building) [1]

19. a) Detailed images are obtained of distance sources (stars, galaxies) [1]; light doesn't have to pass through the atmosphere [1]; which blocks some frequencies [1]

b) **Any two from:** it is hard to repair

[1]; it is expensive to launch [1]; there is a chance of being hit by space debris [1]; there is a chance of damage to the electronics from solar flares [1]; it is difficult to communicate with [1] (Accept any other sensible suggestion)

c) efficiency = $\frac{\text{useful output energy}}{\text{useful input energy}}$ × 100% [1]; = $\frac{300}{1368}$ × 100% [1]; = 21.9% [1] (Accept 0.219)

d) i) Both galaxies are moving away from the Earth [1] (accept telescope); galaxy Y is moving away more quickly than galaxy X [1]

Note that you can't say Y is further away than X, as distance can't be measured directly from red shift. Red shift occurs due to velocity. Think of the change in pitch from a high-speed police car as it passes.

ii) Galaxy Y is moving so quickly that the wavelength of Z has red shifted into the infrared region of the spectrum [1]; the light is no longer visible to the eye / detector [1] (accept: it has been moved into the non-visible part of the spectrum [1]; and can't be seen [1])

20. a) i) Correctly plotted points [1]; with line of best fit (a curve) [1]

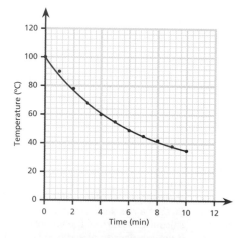

ii) Between 33 and 34°C [1]

iii) Repeat the experiment for several different insulators [1]; conclude that the best insulator has the smallest rate of temperature change [1]

b) i) total energy lost = 6 + 60 + 3 = 69J [1]; electrical energy to the homes = 100 – 69J = 31J per 100J of coal [1]

ii) efficiency = $\frac{\text{useful output energy}}{\text{useful input energy}}$ × 100% [1]; efficiency = $\frac{31}{100}$ × 100% [1]; Efficiency = 31% [1] (Accept 0.31)

21. a) Energy will be lost from the wires due to the heating effect of the current **[1]**

b) i) Transformers only work with an alternating voltage **[1]**

  ii) The current in the 12m wire is very much smaller **[1]**; there is minimal energy loss due to heating **[1]**

> Remember heat lost = I^2R, so keeping the current small is vital to minimise heat losses.

c) i) The ratio of the step-up transformer is 1 : 10 **[1]**; input potential difference = 12V × 10 = 120V **[1]**

  ii) Energy is conserved / power in = power out **[1]**; 12 × 2 = 120 × current, therefore current = 0.2A **[1]**

  iii) That there are no energy losses in the transformer **[1]** (Accept: the transformer is 100% efficient)

22. a) i) 12m/s **[1]**

  ii) Between 12m/s **[1]**; and 16m/s **[1]**

> The gradient of the graph is negative where the output power is falling, as the wind speed increases.

  iii) The output power falls at speeds greater / lower than 12m/s (Accept: or below 12m/s) dimming the lamp **[1]**; OR the lamp would only be at maximum brightness at a wind speed of 12m/s **[1]**

b) i) Any two from: solar panels don't emit greenhouse gases **[1]**; solar panels don't produce particulates **[1]**; solar energy is renewable **[1]**; there are no waste products to be disposed of from solar energy **[1]**; they have a long lifespan, require little maintenance, and can be used in remote areas where there is no mains electricity (or other sensible response) **[1]**

  ii) Any two from: solar cells are expensive to buy **[1]**; large areas of land are needed for high-output solar cells **[1]**; the intensity of sunlight varies during the day and season, and so will the output of the solar panels **[1]**; there is no output from the solar panels at night **[1]**; they are not very attractive to look at (visual pollution) **[1]**; output can be affected by the weather **[1]**

23. a) From the graph: velocity = 12m/s, time = 0.8 seconds **[1]**; distance travelled = 12 × 0.8 = 9.6m **[1]**

b) Change in velocity = 12m/s − 0, time for the change = 0.9 seconds **[1]**; deceleration = $\frac{12}{0.9}$ = 13.3m/s² **[1]**

c) Any one from: a wet road **[1]**; worn brakes **[1]**; worn tyres **[1]**; poor road surface **[1]**; increased load in the car due to passengers **[1]** (or any other suitable answer) **[1]**

d) A graph similar to below, having a longer thinking distance **[1]**; but the **same** braking distance **[1]**

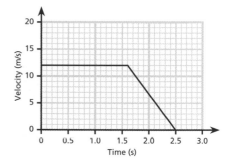

Notes

GCSE Physics Workbook

Notes

Notes

Notes

Notes

Notes

Notes